AGS Management Consultants Pte Ltd

Suite 2305 (24th Storey) Jalan Sultan Centre, Beach Road, Singapore 0719.
Tel: 2923390 Cable: AGSCONSULT Telex: RS 33505 AGS MC

Services Include:

Personnel — Administration
Industrial — Relations
Executive — Search
Staff — Training
Financial — Management
Public — Relations
Market — Research
Marketing — Management
Industrial — Management
Feasibility — Study
Training — Films
Special — Assignments

MESSAGE OF WELCOME

On behalf of AGS Management Consultants Group in Singapore and Malaysia and the Conference Speakers, it is indeed my pleasure and privilege to warmy welcome all of you to attend this two-day international Conference in Singapore on 'Marine Insurance Claims & Frauds'.

This distinguished gathering is even more meaningful because Delegates come from Malaysia, Indonesia, Thailand, Hongkong, Taiwan, Denmark, U.K, USA and Singapore. All of them are from the top and senior management level decision-makers from a variety of companies in shipping, insurance, banking, trading, oil refining and legal practising. Through the change of time, the needs and operations of business activities have become more and more complex. The type of problems arising in the shipping world have also changed from time to time. The recent happenings of marine and commercial frauds all over the world affecting the shipowners, shippers, insurance companies, banks and traders have cause for serious concern due to heavy financial losses and disruption to international trade.

This two-day international Conference on 'Marine Insurance Claims & Frauds' is specially designed to fulfill a felt need to explore ways and means to overcome problems in the shipping world. The complexities of this special subject will be discussed and deliberated by ten distinguished Conference Speakers who are experts in their own fields. They will share with you their knowledge and experiences gained on such matters.

Moreover, about two hundred Delegates from nine countries will have an opportunity to know each other better including the Conference Speakers and Chairmen. The contact established could be very useful indeed.

As Conference Producer, may I wish all of you happy deliberation on such matters and hope you will find the Conference stimualting and beneficial. For those who are from overseas, I would like to wish them a very pleasant stay in Singapore.

Chang Soo
Conference Producer
AGS Management Consultants Pte Ltd
Singapore   November 9, 1981

AGS MANAGEMENT CONSULTANTS SDN. BHD.
32-C Jalan Lumut, Kompleks Damai, Kuala Lumpur 02-13, Malaysia.
Tel: 636939/632882 Cable: GROUPSERVE Telex: MA 30185 AGS

SPEAKERS

Paul Bugden	Solicitor of Supreme Court	Hongkong
Douglas A Cole	Richards Hogg International Average Adjusters Singapore	Singapore
Anthony Colman	Queen's Counsel	London
Charles Haddon-Cave	Barrister-at-Law	London
N K Pillai	Advocate & Solicitor	Singapore
Mrs Judith Prakash	Advocate & Solicitor	Singapore
Capt P J Rivers	Thomas Howell Kiewitt (S) Pte Ltd	Singapore
Jeremy Russell	Barrister-at-Law	London
R J Sayer	Solicitor of Supreme Court UK	London
Capt HP Schulz	A I G	Hongkong

CONTENTS

CONFERENCE PROGRAMME
Monday Nov 9, 1981

Chairman	:	**N K Pillai**
0835	:	**Registration and Coffee**
0900	:	**Opening Address**
		Chung Chee Kit First Deputy Chairman Singapore National Shipowners' Association
		Fu Hua-Zhu Deputy Chairman Singapore National Shippers' Council
0915	:	**Anthony Colman,** Q.C, Opening Speech
0930	:	**RECENT TRENDS IN MARINE FRAUDS** Speaker : R J Sayer
1015	:	**HULL AND CARGO UNDERWRITING** Speaker : Capt H P Schulz
1100	:	**Coffee**
1130	:	**MARINE INSURANCE CLAIMS AND FRAUD** Speaker : Mrs Judith Prakash
1215	:	**SHIP SCUTTLING** Speaker : Charles Haddon-Cave
1300	:	**Lunch**
1430	:	**DOCUMENTARY FRAUD** Speaker : Anthony Colman, Q.C
1515	:	**Tea**
1545	:	**MARINE FRAUD AND ITS PREVENTION** Speaker : Capt P J Rivers
1630	:	**Panel Discussion**
1700	:	**First Day Closing**

CONFERENCE PROGRAMME
Monday Nov 9, 1981

Chairman	N K Pillai	
0835	Registration and Coffee	
0900	Opening Address	
	Chua Chee Kit	
	First Deputy Chairman	
	Singapore National Shippers' Association	
	Fu Hua Zhu	
	Deputy Chairman	
	Singapore National Shipping Council	
0915	Anthony Colman, Q.C. Opening Speech	
0930	RECENT TRENDS IN MARINE FRAUD	
	Speaker: R Grime	
1015	HULL AND CARGO UNDERWRITING	
	Speaker: Capt H E Seifert	
1100	Coffee	
1130	MARINE INSURANCE CLAIMS AND FRAUD	
	Speaker: Mrs Jilani Plakett	
1215	SHIP SCUTTLING	
	Speaker: Charles Haddon-Cave	
1300	Lunch	
1430	DOCUMENTARY FRAUD	
	Speaker: Anthony Colman, Q.C.	
1515	Tea	
1545	MARINE FRAUD AND ITS PREVENTION	
	Speaker: Capt J Rivoli	
1630	Panel Discussion	
1700	First Day Closing	

CONFERENCE PROGRAMME
Tuesday Nov 10, 1981

Chairman	:	**Charles Haddon-Cave**
0915	:	**MARINE INSURANCE CLAIMS AND SHIPS OWNERS' LIABILITY**
		Speaker : N K Pillai
1000	:	**A CASE STUDY FROM HONGKONG**
		Speaker : Paul Bugden
1045	:	**Coffee**
1115	:	**INSURED PERILS, PROXIMATE CAUSE AND MARINE INSURANCE ACT**
		Speaker : Anthony Colman, Q.C
1200	:	**SHIP-OWNERS DEFENCES TO CARGO CLAIMS**
		Speaker : Jeremy Russell
1245	:	**Lunch**
1430	:	**SHIP-OWNERS DEFENCES TO CARGO CLAIMS (Contd)**
1515	:	**Tea**
1545	:	**GENERAL AVERAGE & SALVAGE AND THE EFFECT OF FRAUD**
		Speaker : Douglas A Cole
1630	:	**Panel Discussion**
1700	:	**Close of Conference**

RECENT TRENDS IN MARINE FRAUDS

Speaker: R J Sayer
Solicitor of
Supreme Court, UK
Ince & Co
London

Recent Trends in Marine Frauds

A paper read by Richard Sayer, Solicitor, London.
9.11.81

I shall in the next 45 minutes refer to different types of marine fraud and it might therefore be desirable to start with an attempt at defining the terms I shall use.

I will split the subject into 2 principal parts - wet fraud and dry fraud. Both types may be categorised as marine fraud because they both involve the nomination or charterering or use of a vessel. By dry fraud, I mean fraud which is committed wholly ashore and does not require anybody to get his feet wet or even vaguely damp - you will hear other speakers refer to documentary fraud of charterparty fraud within this definition. By wet fraud, I intend to encompass those cases where the ship is a real part of the plot, rather than merely being a name which has to be inserted in a Bill of Lading or a Letter of Credit.

Therefore I have in mind, within my definition of wet fraud, not only scuttling which is the sinking of the vessel with or without cargo in order to defraud Hull Underwriters and/or with cargo in order to defraud cargo insurers or cargo owners, but also I include those cases where the ship is not necessarily sunk but where at least it purports to be sunk, even if it is, in fact, used subsequently whether it

be for further fraud operations, for refuge transport or for drug running.

Overall trends

Generalising substantially from my experience the following are the clearly discernible trends of marine fraud this century. I say this century merely to put the parameters of the discussion in relatively modern times. Maritime fraud has, of course, taken place ever since the first boat put to sea. Having set the scene by reference to the earlier part of this century I will then concentrate on the way in which there have been recent changes.

For the first 70 years of the century the overwhelming preponderance of cases involving marine fraud was the straight forward hull scuttling. There were certain hallmarks for this type of case. The vessel would be substantially over-insured. It would be very rare to find a vessel of less than third special survey vintage; it would be very rare to find any loss of life or personal injury; the weather, if cheked carefully with independent sources, would be exaggerated to a degree; the vessel would always sink in water sufficiently deep to rule out any prospects of recovery or even of divers examination. Nominal ownership would, of course, be what used to be known as the "Pan-Lib-Hon" variety although beneficial ownership would usually be Mediterranean which would also be the nationality of most of the officers and a lot of the crews. It became, from an investigator's viewpoint a badge of the scuttling case to

find that the vessel's deck log and sometimes other logs as well had been lost in the rescue of the crew. The logs were always lost in exactly the same way and I always wondered whether there was, in fact, a publication entitled "Do's and Don'ts for scuttling Masters", in which the loss of the logs was covered in Chapter 4. The standard explanation in the Master's statement was in the following lines:

"I went into the Wheelhouse and got the working chart and the deck log, put them in a plastic bag which I gave to the Second Mate and told him to look after them if we abandoned. Later when I had given the order to abandon ship, I saw the Second Mate ahead of me pass the plastic bag down into the lifeboat which was moored to the bottom of the pilot ladder. Unfortunately, just as he let go of the bag, the boat was caught by a wave, swung away from the ladder and the bag fell into the water - never to be seen again."

Ironically what has subsequently happened is that one meets the same tragic story of the loss of log book in so many total loss cases - even those which are plainly innocent total losses - that it has now become almost a badge of innocence rather than fraud.

During the first 70 years of the century whilst the vast majority of cases were hull scuttlings, there were, of course, cases of wet fraud involving cargo. For example, the case of the ship which was going to be sunk which was found to have crates of stones for a cargo rather than crates of jade pieces. There were also limited examples of

3

what has subsequently became a trend time charterers who disappear after collecting freight and before paying hire, - but they were few and far between. Marine fraud in those days was essentially of the classical kind in which the ship went down allegedly as a result of striking the famous, ubiquitous, submerged floating object, which we all know sails the oceans of the world looking for old, over-insured vessel to run into, or alternatively, as a result of very heavy weather, causing unexpected leakage in three of the vessels holds and engineroom - all at the same time.

Sinking was probably the most popular method, but Stranding was a close second. You don't have to make the ship disappear to establish a total loss claim: a constructive Total Loss will produce the same amount of cash. As long as the Stranding was at a good speed on a rocky bottom, and as a bonus if it damaged the expensive steering gear, there was a good chance that the repair cost would exceed the insured value. A sinking immediately alerts the suspicious insurer - particularly if the story is one of water appearing in several allegedly watertight compartments at the same time - whereas a Stranding will give the investigator a hard time : the compass or radar will have failed - but that is not evidence of fraud - and there will have been poor visibility and some negligence in navigation. A careful Stranding Story will be more difficult to crack than a Sinking Story, however carefully presented.

If we follow that line a little further we will find

the fire case: it is always astonishing to me that fire, difficult to control and horrible in its effect on the human body, can be chosen as a method of marine fraud. But chosen it is and not infrequently.

Thereafter we get to the less usual methods. One that is worth mentioning is that of deliberate machinery damage. The casual observer might be forgiven for thinking that a machinery damage claim is unlikely to be of interest to a fraudsman. However, as soon as one realises that the engines are the most valuable part of a result and that severe damage to bearings and shafts by an engineer interrupting the lubrication feed for even a short period - can produce a CTL then one will be aware that one does'nt have to sink or even strand a ship to effect a fraud on underwriters.

Dry fraud existed, but it was so far as one could tell sporadic and limited in popularity, although the point must be made that in those days there was very little publicity of fraud such as exists today and therefore there may in fact have been a thriving industry but which was invisible to students of the art.

One case I came across demonstrates how astonishingly easy it can sometimes be for a fraudster to dupe his victim if the victim fails to exercise common sense. A shipowning firm who became a public Company in U.S.A. began to run into financial trouble and desperate to obtain further bank finance discovered a very easy way of doing so. They formed two $100 Liberian corporations - one called something like

Mobil Oil of Liberia Inc., and the other something like BP of Liberia Inc. They then drew up 2 time charters in profitable terms between themselves and these companies as charterers and presented them to their bankers as evidence of the fact that their vessels, which were mortgaged to the bank, were supported by profitable income from first class charterers. The banks, suitably impressed, extended further lines of credit to the owners.

The Non-Fraud case

So far I have been talking about frauds which have occurred. As a change let us look briefly at the frauds which do not occur but which someone fraudulently wishes to suggest did occur. By this, I mean cases where Underwriters are approached either directly by crew members of through a third party who acts as an information broker, with the promise of the "true story" of why the Good Ship "Lollypop" sank three weeks ago. The informant advises that he can offer solid proof of the fact that the sinking was deliberate, and ordered by the ship owners, but of course he will not reveal his full story till some "understanding" has been reached with Underwriters as to his expenses. Now it is at this point that the Investigator really earns his money. He has to be able to judge whether this is a canary who is prepared to sing a true, straightforward song or, on the otherhand, is merely a parrot who is about to repeat a well-rehearsed series of lines borne of the imagination rather than of fact. The investigator will be well advised

6

to bypass the informant and to concentrate his enquiries elsewhere for no underwriter should fight a case merely on the back of information supplied by an informant in these circumstances. The trend which has seen an increase in the numbers of marine fraud cases in the last few years has it appears produced a similar increase in the number of instances of ship's witnesses professing marine fraud where there has been none.

I can quote as a somewhat amusing example of this, a personal experience from a year or two ago. In the course of investigating a loss in behalf of hull Underwriters I was invited together with Underwriters Greek Lawyer to meet the vessel's master for a private discussion. We fixed the meeting for the lobby of a large Athens hotel where we sat listening to the master's tale of how he wished to cooperate with us in revealing the true story. Fortunately, rather than looking continually into the clear blue honest eyes of the master I was able to spot that a man who was sitting in an armchair facing away from us about 30 feet distant and who had apparently been casually testing his camera by pointing it in directions other than ours, had placed his camera on the arm of the chair pointing at us whilst he looked away from us. My Greek lawyer colleague thought I had taken leave of my senses when I politely asked the master if he would ask the unknown gentleman sitting in the distant armchair to join us for a drink. This request was finally granted and midst great embarasssment the stranger joined us and I asked why he had photographed us. I am sorry to say this completely failed to produce anything remotely ressembling a theatrical admission that he had been

caught in the act and offers to go quietly with us to the police station. Apparently that only happens to James Bond. Instead there was blank amazement all round and muttered discussion in Greek obviously to the effect that the unfortunate Englishman had suddenly got a bad case of sunstroke which had affected his brain. I made profuse apologies and bought everyone a drink, knowing that the point had been made and the Master now knew that I knew we had been photographed.

The end of the story was that my Greek lawyer tracked the man down subsequently and found that he was as ex member of the Greek CIA who had been employed by the master to photograph him talking to the underwriters lawyers so that the master could present the photo to the shipowners with his demand for money for changing his allegiance from underwriters to the owners.

On further investigation we were able to satisfy ourselves that this was a completely innocent loss and underwriters paid in full shortly thereafter.

Having strayed on to the topic of investigation of fraud, and without wishing to take any thunder from Phil Rivers who will be talking about investigation, I will mention a couple of points. Whilst the investigator may only have to concentrate on a few members of the crew as the others were not in on the act, some of the best leads can be obtained from uninvolved crew members. In a very recent celebrated case a crucial witness turned out to be the assistant Cook who recounted how he had been ordered to

prepare sandwiches rather than a cooked meal, and only appreciated the significance of it when he found himself eating his share of the sandwiches in the ships lifeboat whilst watching the ship slowly sinking half a mile distant.

Whilst on the topic of "uninvolved" crew members there can be little doubt which crewman holds the record for being least involved in a sinking. One of my colleagues was puzzled to find that the rescuing vessel reported having picked up 15 survivors but the owners lawyer had interviewed and produced statements for 16 survivors. The truth only came out some time later : after the casualty the owners had sought out and obtained, no doubt at same expense, a certificated master who had been flown out to the port where the survivors had landed and had there presented himself to owners lawyer as the master of the casualty. It was our good fortune and the owners bad luck that another master whom the owners had first approached to act as the stand -in for statement purposes but who had declined to do so, was the brother-in-law of one of our Greek correspondents partners, to whom he told the tale.

That trend is one which we could all do without.

Recent Changes

I have sofar dealt with the general trend of the first 70 years of the century. What has changed since?

In my view 2 things have happened :

Firstly the incidence of marine fraud has increased,

9

and

Secondly the emphasis has altered : the cargo rather than the hull has become increasingly but not in all cases the primary motivation for the fraudsman.

Firstly the increase. The incidence of marine fraud has always been cyclical. In broad terms ships go down as the freight market goes down, and although there are exceptions it has been relatively rare for there to be a large number of sinkings(and I must stress that I am here concentrating on Wet fraud) when the freight market is booming. Now I believe that cyclical aspect has changed somewhat. One suggestion I can put forward for this is that in the old days the fraudsmen were usually shipowners who when suffering from the periodic recessionary trend in the freight market would in desperation turn to fraud. Today however, the increase in dry fraud has brought non-shipping men into the scene. There are also new Socio - political factors - such as the civil war in the Lebanon and its resulting opportunities for clandestine trading, and the Vietnamese disasters with its consequent awful refuge export trade, which have brought into the marine world the worst elements of the non-marine criminal society. These then are not Shipowners who seek to make money from shipping when the freight market is good but get tempted into fraud when it turns bad, they are fraudsmen who have turned to shipping as a new outlet for their fraudulent plans. Whatever the reasons may be there has undoubtedly been an increase in the last 10 years.

Secondly the emphasis has altered so that cargo fraud,

whether wet or dry, has become more prevalent than straight hull fraud. There are still cases of sinkings, fires, strandings and the like where the cargo is not an integral part of the plot, but they are limited. The cargo emphasis is puzzling - not because it has occurred now, but that it did'nt occur (to the same extent) before. There have always been high value cargoes carried on low value ships - the motive has always been there. What has perhaps changed has been the increase in the world seaborne trade of finished goods : as an example take the vast values which can be accumulated in a full shipload of tape recorders, cassettes televisions etc. .

The trend towards cargo fraud covers both dry and wet fraud. The dry area has developed vastly in recent years : in many cases that is arguably not even marine fraud as the connection with the sea and with shipping can be peripheral - it is export/import or sale of goods fraud. However the insurers are of course the marine insurers. The perpetrators of such frauds are usually not shipping people. In the old days the perpetrator would be the shipowner who might contemplate bringing in a cargo shipper or consignee in a joint venture. These days the perpetrator is quite likely to be a businessman in export/import, who connives with his business collegues on dry fraud, but for wet fraud he must go into the market place and seek out a shipowner or at least someone with substantial shipping experience. Therein lies one of the great difficulties for the wet cargo fraudsman: the involvement of a lot of people. A hull fraud need only involve the shipowner and 2 or 3 crewmen. The investigator will be aware of the fact that he may only

11

be concerned, in a sinking case, with the second engineer or oiler, with one deck officer and perhaps the radio officer. As the Glory Universe case shows the master may not be privy to the original plot. However the wet cargo fraud adds a string of parties : the "document doctor" for example must procure Bills of Lading, warehouse receipts, mate's receipts, tallies, survey reports in some cases, apart from covering the invoices, packing lists and the Letter of - credit formalities.

The document doctor's job must at all times be a frustrating one. In a recent Far East case the Bills of Lading which were printed for the vessel which was about to be used for a sinking came back from the printers with a typing error in the ship's name. It was too late to get them altered and no doubt various oaths were uttered as the fraudsmen had to change the name of the ship to this rather odd mispelt name.

I will not go further into documentary fraud the delights of which will shortly be propounded by Tony Colman.

The trend towards joint hull/cargo wet fraud is a very disturbing one. As the Ferit findings demonstrated, it is only when the claims records of all insurers in the whole region are collected together can the shape and size of such a trend be appreciated. Until that is done individual insurers can only guess whether of not their own particular loss experience is part of a new and concentrated pattern of fraud. Ferit found clear links between apparently completely separate losses. Shipowners in one case were

found to be cargo interests in another case. Charterers in one case were discovered as Shipowners or agents in another. Cargo interests were found to have had involvement in 4, 5, or 6 different casualties. The individual investigators in individual cases could not, in advance of a Ferit type cooperative effort, be expected to be aware of such links - although some by dint of a mixture of hard work and a good memory did uncover substantial parts of the overall jigsaw.

The other disturbing aspect of the hull/cargo fraud trend is the size of the individual case. It is bad enough for Far East underwriters to be faced with cargo claims of $10 million per vessel but that is overshadowed by cases like the Salem where the fraudsters used a big ship and a big cargo worth more that $50 million. There has since then been another fraud involving a large tanker sinking with an alleged full cargo of oil which upon investigation was found to hve been discharged at an intermediate port, and we must all hope that the culprits in both cases will be shortly brought to justice as a deterrent to this unwelcome trend of large vessel frauds.

So far as the Far East is concerned although I have been London based since the Ferit enquiry ended I have kept in close contact with developments in the region - the trend has moved away from hull/cargo wet frauds and into the dry fraud area. Leaving aside Letter of Credit documentary fraud which will be covered by later speakers, let us look at 2 examples of dry fraud :-

The Charterparty Fraud

The Charterparty fraud is essentially a simple operation in which the fraudster is the charterer. He may also, in some cases, be the owner as well, but in heavy disguise. He charters either from himself or from an innocent outsider, on a short time charter. He pays the first half month's hire as required by the charter, and loads the cargo. The ship sails for the destination he has ordered. When 15 days have elapsed he fails to pay the next half-month's hire and the owner finds the charterer's office has closed and the charterer has disappeared, taking with him the prepaid freight which he has collected from the cargo owners. The shipowner is defrauded of the unpaid hire and of the discharging costs unless he is able to persuade the very irate consignee to pay a second freight to cover these items.

The Freight diversion fraud

A variant of the Charterparty fraud has recently appeared. It goes like this: innocent and reputable owners are put into contact with innocent reputable charterers by the fraudster who plays the role of a broker. The Charterers load the cargo and prepare to pay the freight. They are given remittance instructions by the fraudster - who they believe to be a straightforward broker and with whom they expect to communicate direct (rather than with the shipowner) as customary. They pay into the bank account nominated by the fraudster and are astonished and dismayed to find a few days later a direct request from the owner for

14

information as to why they have not paid. It is then discovered that the "broker" was a fraud and had departed with the freight.

If you are a shipping man rather than an insurer, the moral of these tales is the same - be careful with whom you do business or you may lose your shirt - and no doubt your trousers as well after the expensive Lawyers have had their go at the case.

Trends in the Prevention of Marine Fraud

Having been involved in the Ferit exercise I felt that it might be useful if based upon that experience I mentioned a few points in respect of the trend in the prevention of marine fraud.

(1)   Most frauds involve insurance thus it is an evident truth that if insurers do everything they reasonably can to avoid paying fraudulent claims this will provide a massive disincentive to future fraud.   That is of course easy to say but difficult to achieve as underwriters are not policemen, they are businessmen.   However, there are things that insurers can do which will not involve great expense and will not be too disruptive to their everyday business.

First as the Ferit exercise showed, insurers can and should share information amongst themselves.   I appreciate that insurance is a highly competitive matter and competitors do not

readily share their secrets. But there can be no benefit to an individual insurer in secreting information about a fraud which has been perpetrated upon that insurer or about which he has obtained advice.

If insurers are prepared to share such information, how in practice can they best do so ? It is not for me, a non-insurer, to answer this question, but as someone interested in seeking to eliminate marine fraud - as indeed we all are - I would with apologies for my temerity, put forward some suggestions. One way of collating this intelligence could be for each MIA within the region to form a small liaison committee to promote and to gather the exchange of information between its members - rather like in the London market the weekly claims adjusters meetings. The information gathered by that liaison committee could then be passed to a regional body which would store it and disseminate it back to the individual national Associations with or without recommendations for action.

When insurers meet a suspicious case they must, to give themselves a fair chance do two things : one is to instruct their investigator immediately - for the trail will go cold quickly. The second is to tap the information already in existence as the result of the exchange of intelligence to which I have already referred.

That means they can pick up the phone and ask the regional body - which currently has been Ferit - for any data available about the people and companies involved in the case they are now investigating.

You may ask whether a data bank such as that really has any practical value. I will give you just two instances from the Ferit enquiry and you can answer the question yourselves:

We were essentially investigating losses which had occurred in the previous couple of years or so prior to the creation of Ferit. I am talking of 1976 - 79. We discovered numerous examples of repeat frauds where the same individuals had been involved either in ownership of ships or cargoes or as crew members on different losses.

As a long shot I asked my London office to dig into the archives for details of the personnel involved in four Far East losses which we had investigated for London insurers between 1959 and 1963. Much to our surprise this revealed :

Firstly, a third engineer who had been involved as 2nd engineer and Chief engineer in two of the Ferit losses 19 years later.

Secondly a crew member who was 19 years later a shareholder in one of the Ferit ships.

And thirdly an owner who had so far as we could ascertain retired from the fraud business only to reappear 16 years later.

Now any investigator worth his salt will when interviewing the crew members, list, hopefully by reference to the seaman's discharge book, all vessels upon which the crewman has previously served, in the hope of throwing up previous suspicious casualties which he can check from Lloyd's confidential information, but he has no way of checking the crewmember's history if he has no access to the data banks such as exist in London and with Ferit. If he does have access then it will not be of much value if those data banks are not kept updated : the time which insurers need spend on such updating is entirely minimal, but the benefit could be substantial.

Those are some thoughts in trends in prevention by insurers, and the development of those trends.

(2) I turn now to the police. There has been a distinctive trend towards involvement of the police by the commercial interests in marine fraud cases. It used to be said that insurers did not involve the police and therefore were not helping to stamp out the menace of fraud.

I believe that the greatest deterrent to

marine fraud is the prosecution of the fraudsters. The police must therefore be brought in. In recent years the trend has changed and I do not consider that the commercial interests can today be criticised for failing to share their troubles with the criminal authorities. I have seen many cases, particularly in the Far East, where insurers have been quite prepared to file a complaint and have thereafter liaised with the police. However, I would respectfully suggest that some improvement can still be made in those lines of communication. For example all countries in the region would do well to follow the example of Singapore in creating a committee at which representatives of the police authorities and the commercial interests sit together. An informal committee on marine matters exists between members of the Union of Greek Shipowners and the Salvage Association on behalf of the London insurance market. Somewhat similar bodies exist in other fields: for example the California Insurance Department Fraud Bureau recently reported that more than 3,500 instances of suspected fraud involving at least $50 million have been referred to the State by insurance company investigators in California in the last 2½ years. Legislation in New York has recently created an Insurance Fraud Bureau to bridge the gap between the civil and criminal investigators.

There is no doubt that the most effective

means of uncovering a fraud is for the commercial investigator and the police to work together. The former will have his sources of information, his expertise in the specialised field, his contacts in the industry and his ability to spot a fraud by interviewing the witnesses in day one. On the other hand he does not have the power as do the police in appropriate cases to enter and search, to seize documents and to interrogate witnesses who are not prepared to meet him. They can each do their own job and given absolute mutual trust can pool their respective skills to the common benefit.

Thus any forum, such as a national liaison committee or an international regional body already mentioned which will improve cooperation between the commercial interests and the police can in my view only be a step in the right direction.

Conlusion

It may well be that I have given the impression that marine fraud has grown, will continue to grow and that the future for the shipping and insurance industries is a bleak one. If so, then I wish to correct that impression. It is my view that with the increasing incidence of successful prosecutions - in which Singapore deserves great credit, and with the greater viligance which is being displayed by commercial parties marine fraud is being beaten. I hope

that some of the ideas which this conference will provoke
will assist in maintaining that trend.

HULL AND CARGO UNDERWRITING

Speaker: Capt H P Schulz
Asst Vice-President
A I G
Hongkong

HULL & CARGO UNDERWRITING

(With special emphasis on fraud prevention)

Paper written and read by Capt. H.P. Schulz

THIS SEMINAR, I am confident, will contribute to the prevention of maritime fraud. The increased awareness of the problem, and the specific information and suggestions on how to tackle this problem and avoid becoming a victim, are the two most important factors in fighting this sort of crime.

As for my part, I have been asked by the organisers to talk about underwriting : Marine Hull and Cargo. Surely it was not expected that we have half an hour or so of lecturing in general underwriting practices and discuss clauses etc. or give a list of points the underwriter has to observe when dealing with a risk offered to him, but it may be worthwhile to touch on a few items of general nature and history of marine underwriting. This may show us how and why the situation has changed in recent years and what the experienced and careful underwriter of today now has to consider in addition to what he was used to.

The shipping industry greatly depended and still depends on "bona fide" transactions. For every party in this business, the ship-owner, the shipper, the charterers, the insurers and everybody else connected with this industry, the word of mouth has been equally binding as the written contract or agreement.

This was and still is so in all parts of the world with people of different nationalities. The system and procedures of maritime trade and related industries were created on this basis, heavily relying on trust and confidence and the integrity of the business partners. This system with all its institutions has worked well for a long time, but is it still adequate? My personal opinion is that the system has given the modern pirate the opportunity, almost under the eyes of the world and our authorities, to develop his line of business to perfection. I hate to say it, but our modern society accepts and tolerates that business is done with unscrupulous people. Where profit can be expected even an honest man does not ask too many questions anymore. This change in attitude appears to be the fundamental change we have to take into consideration when we do our underwriting job, be it hull or cargo.

Having said this, one may get the impression that underwriting of marine risks was easier some 20 or even 50 years ago. It was not really easier but less complicated as the majority of business offered in those days was of better quality with less moral hazard. The marine exposure used to be the natural elements, the perils of the sea, the stranding, sinking and heavy weather damage. It was difficult for the underwriter to obtain the order for a risk or a share of it. Today I sometimes get the impression that it should be the other way around, that is, that it should be difficult to place some business through a competent underwriter with a reputable

insurance company. In general it can be said that the majority of claims are caused by the human being, no longer by the elements.

Our text-books teaching us the principles of marine insurance tell us that it is the insurer who has to make up his mind whether or not be accepts the risk offered and at what rate. The handbooks also say that the underwriter has to base his judgement on the underwriting information given to him by the prospective client or by the broker. It appears unreasonable that the insurer goes to examine the goods prior to shipment and also makes sure that they are being shipped and consequently the insurance contract is made on the principle of good faith . The Insurance Act of 1906 in Section 17 states that a contract of marine insurance is a contract based upon the utmost good faith to be observed by both parties of such contract.

What is the information we, the underwriters, wanted to know from the proposer and the broker to make up our minds to accept the business or not? For a cargo policy, let's assume a one shot deal, we ask for a description of the goods, the packing, the value, place or origin and final destination, means of transportation, previous experience and the carrying vessel's name. With this basic information the underwriter sat down and used his experience. He knows that this type of cargo is either liable to pilferage or spontaneous combustion. He knows about the loading facilities at the shipping port and if necessary checks about the equipment at the port of

destination. He knows that the North Atlantic in winter is rough and that this cargo is going to be taken through 2 or 3 different climate zones and could suffer sweat-water damage. He finally puts everything together, comes up with a rate which he feels is adequate and hopes it is competitive under market conditions. However, he may not like the risk because his company has previously had poor experience with this kind of commodity or some other valuable reason. It sounds simple and if one had the experience and knows the technicalities of marine insurance, it <u>was</u> relatively easy.

The principles of hull insurance are not so different. The underwriting information is : We want to know about the valuation of hull and machinery, or top values if we have a fleet, age and where built, trading pattern and geographical limits, crew and management, loss history, classification and a few other things. In many cases, we even send our surveyors to carry out a pre-acceptance survey. In general, we are taking bigger money on the hull side and the basic underwriting information is more detailed and the various registers enable us to even verify such information, but still <u>trust</u> and <u>good faith</u> prevail over all our actions in marine insurance.

Both today and tomorrow we will hear about maritime fraud, the techniques and various forms of it, and I believe it will become

very clear that we, the marine insurers, will not be able to continue to underwrite in the way I described earlier and be guided only by our checklist of information. Additional criterias need to be added to this list and we need to take more initiative ourselves. People have advised us and our bosses have told us to be more careful in our underwriting. The question is how? What are we expected to do to avoid being trapped and becoming involved in a fraudulent case. I know we will be unable to eliminate maritime fraud and occasionally we will be caught again, but there are a few points where I think we, the insurance people, can do a little better or at least can do something more to protect ourselves from getting involved in such cases of maritime fraud.

Earlier I mentioned a few of the basic underwriting criteria for hull insurances as well as cargo. Hopefully underwriters never forget to obtain this information and look at the size of the vessel, classification etc. but it is not enough to only have these data and then not work with them. If one has the vessel's name and the port of loading, for example, one may find out that the vessel is presently sailing in another ocean at the time when the Bill of Lading is issued. We should never forget to take the elementary precautions of checking the Bill of Lading quantity against the vessel's loading capacity. The underwriters and everyone in the industry who usually only sees documents and obtain information has to undertake those simple basic day-to-day checks before he takes any action and makes

decisions. When investigating suspicious claims, especially during the last 3 years or so, I have seen those basic underwriting principles being neglected. I have seen policies issued for large shipments of colour television sets to certain developing countries which did not have colour televised at that time at all. I mention this basic point only to remind the underwriter of his importance and to appeal to everybody to make use of that information to prudently judge if a risk is acceptable or not. It is so easy to slide into a routine and collect the information on the check-list and do nothing with them.

Times, however, have changed and modern techniques have made a lot of things easier in our lives. Those modern techniques and equipment have also made it easier to arrange for fraud, documents can easily be forged and modern communication features help to decide when and where the criminal act is to be carried out. The underwriters, I feel, have to adjust to this situation and not only consider the physical aspects of a risk to be underwritten but put the utmost importance on information about the "human factor". Unfortunately, only too often, very little is known and asked about those "human aspects" of a risk, most likely because this type of information is difficult to obtain. If our marine portfolio is to remain profitable, or has to be returned to profitability, we cannot afford to neglect the search for information about our prospective clients. This, by all means, does not mean that we are suspicious or do not believe in honest and straightforward business and we do not want to interfere with somebody's business practices, but we

have to know more about the general business profile of a
shipowner, ship management or operator of a vessel, or a shipper
or consignee of some cargo.

Allow me a few minutes to go into a little more detail in this
connection as far as the hull underwriting is concerned. I used
the phrase of the "general business profile". This does not only
consist of the financial background but when we know that the
executive management of such company is well versed and experienced
in shipping matters we should feel a little better. The up-keeping
of the vessel or the fleet is another factor to collect information
about and so is the employment of competent officers and crews at
a proper wage level. Underpaid crews tend to compensate this
deficiency somehow. A shipowner's shore management is of great
importance, the administration and planning, the securing of
reliable cargo sources for constant freight income. I am aware
that it is not easy to obtain such information and very often it
is not possible to get all we really would like to have. Simply the
grade of difficulty one may encounter to collect such information
can be an underwriting criteria. Usually well managed and professional
shipowners or managers readily provide such information to identify
their shipping and trade operations. This also applies to cargo
underwriting to a certain degree.

A very effective way to fill gaps in information is the underwriting
survey. A physical inspection of the vessel to be insured, or even

a sister ship or other vessel of a fleet if any, by a
professional surveyor usually helps tremendously to prudently
judge the acceptability of such risk. The appointed surveyor
could easily include one or the other brief interview with officers
and crew members and pay a visit to the respective shore office and
report accordingly. Such a survey does cost money and I can see
the objections with extremely tightly calculated rates and ever-
growing overhead expenses. On the hull side, we usually deal
with big sums of money and I firmly believe that a few extra dollars
spent in time can keep us all out of a lot of trouble. In fact a
few extra dollars spent on a survey could mean a few cents off
your premium rate, obviously this is an address to the shipowners
present. I think I could also address the shippers at this point:
Choose your shipping line carefully and let your insurer know. A
few extra cents on the freight rate can save you not only problems
but money on your insurance premium.

An old friend of mine said during a similar conference in New York
last year and I am sure he does not mind me quoting him here,
"It is unwise to pay too much, but it is worse to pay too little.
When you pay too little, you sometimes lose everything, because
the thing you bought was incapable of doing whatever it was bought
to do."

In general the same concept applies to cargo underwriting. Usually
the sums insured are by far smaller than those in hull but every

dollar counts and has to be accounted for. I emphasize again the importance of evaluation of a client's business operation as a whole before quoting rates and conditions on a specific shipment. It is relatively more difficult to obtain the required information for cargo insurances simply because one theoretically would have to look at both parties; the shipper and the consignee. If we insure imports into the country where we operate as insurers we can exercise certain controls over the cargo and usually know the importer. We could even arrange outturn surveys and superintendence surveys for certain cargoes but exported goods leave for a certain destination which could be a remote place somewhere at the other side of the globe. It appears to me very useful to have the consignee's full name and address and if you have a contact or even an office nearby the destination to confirm the existence of the consignee.

All this sounds as if we the insurers have to train our underwriters to become policemen or insurance detectives or even spies to spend most of their time to investigate and obtain company searches from the registrar's office. Surely this is not so and not every quotation makes such extensive research necessary. And wanting to know about somebody's business profile and practices does not mean questioning the credibility. It is nothing else than wanting to know who one does business with. The shipper or shipowner surely also wants to know how good, efficient and solvent

his insurer is.

I would like to conclude my remarks about the underwriting
criteria with a word about the claims managers. They do know the
questions to ask and how to mount investigations to hopefully
identify and separate the good guys from the bad ones. They,
however, usually only come into the picture when it is too late
when we have a loss and a problem. If the underwriters decide to
do some of their investigation work before we put a risk on our
books it should prove worthwhile.

I have heard the argument that underwriters should tighten
their underwriting and exercise control by incorporating clauses
and warranties in their policies. I have not seen any clauses or
policy conditions which could prevent fraud. To try to tackle the
problem from the underwriter's desk leads to nothing but overall,
the standards have to be improved.

Nobody can give even a reasonably accurate estimate by how much
underwriters were defrauded, let us say, during the last 3-4 years.
All we know is that it is big money, very big money. The man in
the street, the individual in our offices may know about one or
another spectacular fraud case but he believes that marine fraud
does not affect him. It does not affect him directly but fraud of
this size contributes to inflation. The immediate losers seem
to be the insurance companies, the importers and exporters. But

"what is lost today will be the surcharge of tomorrow" and ultimately our man in the street, our underwriter himself, the average consumer, pays. We, as insurers, have a responsibility to our premium-paying clients and underwriters should be motivated and encouraged to fight this type of inflation. Accusations and critics saying that modern piracy serves the purpose to justify raising rates are false. The insurers have been the victims of marine fraud, not the beneficiaries. I have no doubt that the insurers can do a lot better to protect themselves but we can generally all do a much better job of advising our clients about the dangers of marine fraud. We used to offer advice after the fact, after the claim was filed, but I see no reason why we should not tell them what warning signs to look for so that the client can act accordingly, at least reduce his potential risk.

Marine fraud is a complicated problem for underwriters and all other parties in the shipping industry and I do not pretend to have the answers on what should and can be done to solve it. What appears to me the most important weapon to fight this type of crime is cooperation. What I am going to say about cooperation may provoke some nasty comments and I feel I should start apologizing now if I offend anybody.

There is a serious need for better cooperation among the insurance companies. Experience has shown that many insurers have been ripped off by the same people and in spite of this fact it appears that various insurers guard the information and results of

investigations rather than sharing them. We are competitors all right but we have to jointly defend our image and paying suspicious claims does not enhance this image and it is not in the best interest of our clients as well.

The insurance industry made the first steps to joint action in 1979 when the Far East Regional Investigation Team was formed. This action was taken because of the rising toll of vessels foundering in the South China Sea and claims running into the millions of U.S dollars and insurers were desperate. Now, two years later, which were reasonably quiet in S/E Asia as far as marine fraud is concerned, we seem to slide back into the old pattern of minding our own business and problems. I hope these last two years are not the calm before a new storm, but if insurers keep guarding information or are afraid or even ashamed to tell others that they have been caught, we are opening the doors again for the modern pirates. We are not powerless if we decide to struggle individually but we are powerful if we cooperate with each other and the various authorities. I even go a step further and propose cooperation of the whole shipping industry. The shipping company, the carrier, is not the cargo insurer's natural enemy although we are often fighting over recoveries and third party liability claims. The honest shipowner is as interested as insurers in cracking down on shipping fraud. A coordinated campaign launched by the shipping industry will finally convince the police forces everywhere in the world that marine fraud is a serious crime.

HULL & CARGO UNDERWRITING

And finally, I believe that the publicity, the public awareness is of tremendous importance. A year ago there was hardly any of our technical magazines which did not have an article about marine fraud and it is very encouraging to see that there is still a great interest as this seminar shows. I am confident that we all will come closer to a solution if we continue to exchange our ideas. I appreciate to have been given the opportunity to present my views and be part of this international undertaking to find weaknesses of our industry and ways to protect ourselves. Thank you.

I will be glad to answer questions which you may have about my remarks.

(This paper expresses the personal views of the speaker).

MARINE INSURANCE CLAIMS AND FRAUD

Speaker: **Mrs Judith Prakash**
Advocate & Solicitor
Singapore

MARINE INSURANCE CLAIMS AND FRAUD

By Mrs Judith Prakash

The purpose of my paper today is to give a brief outline of the various kinds of frauds that can be perpetrated by persons holding marine insurance policies, in particular, shipowners or other persons interested in the vessel, for example, the master and crew and mortgagees; and cargo owners whether shippers or consignees. The liability of the insurer when fraud is ascertained will also be discussed. It might surprise you to know that there are situations where even though the loss of either ship or the cargo has been caused by fraud, the insurer is still liable to pay under the policy to the person who has lost the ship or his cargo.

The basic law governing marine insurance in Singapore is the English Marine Insurance Act 1906 together with various cases which have been decided both in England and in SIngapore. It might be pertinent to go to a few sections of the Marine Insurance Act before I continue with this lecture.

First of all, according to Section 1 of the Act, a contract of marine insurance is defined as a contract whereby the insurers undertake to indemnify the assured in manner and to extent whereby agreed against marine losses that is to say, the losses incident to marine adventure. The words 'Marine Adventure' are said in the Act to particularly refer to a situation where any ship, goods or other movables are exposed to marine perils. Marine perils or maritime perils are defined to include the perils consequent on or incident to navigation of the sea. That is, perils of the sea, fire, war perils, pirates, robbers, thieves, captures, seizures, restraint and detainment

of princes and people, jettison and barratry and other similar peril
or perils which are designated by the policy.

In relation to fraud, it must be noted that Section 17 of the Marine Insurance
Act expressly provides that a marine insurance contract is a contract
of utmost good faith and if this utmost good faith is not observed by either
party, the other may declare the contract to be void and of null effect.
Allied with this provision is Clause 18 of the Act which imposes upon
the assured the duty to make full disclosure of every material circumstance
relating to the risk when applying for a marine insurance policy.

The sections which I have just quoted form the basis of the marine insurers'
protection in the case of fraud which is the antithesis of the principles
as found in the Section. The party practising the fraud clearly departs
from the duty of utmost good faith and as a result the insurer is entitled
quite apart from any criminal liability that may rest with the fraudster
to repudiate his responsibility under the contract of insurance immediately.

It is sad but true to say as has been discussed by Mr Sayer that the incidence
of marine fraud has grown enormously over the past few years. This
is particularly true in Singapore where there has been an escalation from
a number of small time frauds to frauds of great complexity involving
months of planning and millions of dollars.

The marine insurance frauds that I wish to discuss can be broken down
into 2 main categories : Hull and cargo frauds. The recent sophisticated
schemes that have surfaced are a combination of the hull fraud and the
cargo fraud.

I would first like to discuss the various types of cargo frauds. These range from the completely fraudulent transaction in which no goods are shipped at all but a marine insurance policy is applied for to the more petty frauds where the owner exaggerate the loss or damage sustained by the cargo. Some of these frauds are so common place that the persons perpetrating them do not consider themselves as acting fraudulently at all. After all, as they say, everyone does it and if we did not, we would be out of business.

The commonest frauds involve obtaining a Bill of Lading which is incorrect in a material particular or which omits some vital information. These frauds are generally the result of the Letter of Credit payment system. The frauds can be categorized as follows : First, there is the case where the shipper of cargo obtains from the shipping agency a shipped Bill of Lading that is antedated. That means that the Bill of Lading purports to show that the cargo has been loaded onto a particular vessel as at the date of the Bill of Lading when in fact no cargo has been loaded at all. The cargo may be in the godown awaiting shipment but the shipper is constrained by the terms of the Letter of Credit to get a Bill of Lading immediately so that he can negotiate the Letter of Credit before it expires.

Sometimes, shippers face genuine difficulties when vessels are delayed and buyers refuse to extend their Letter of Credit and perhaps one would not treat this type of fraud very seriously, but the fact does remain that this method of solving the shippers' problem does border on the fraudulent because what happens is that the bank is deceived into paying money for

the goods which allegedly have been shipped when the ship has not arrived and the goods have been at the dock all along. In one case which I am aware of, what happened was in fact that the Bill of Lading was negotiated, the bank paid the shipper, the buyer paid the bank, and the ship sank before it ever came to SIngapore. So the goods in the end had to be shipped on another vessel and they were lost during transit. What is the position of the insurance company where the Bill of Lading has been antedated? The fraud if any, is not directed at the insurer : as I said earlier, the goods actually exist but will be shipped somewhat later. I am of the view that as long as the goods are eventually shipped in the vessel named in the Bill of Lading or if there is a change of vessel and this is communicated to the insurer and accepted by the insurer, the insurer would be responsible for any loss or damage to the goods during the period of transit. This is because the goods actually exist and the insurance could have attached to the goods as, generally, by terms of the marine insurance policy the insurance attaches to the goods at the time they leave the supplier's storehouse on the course of their transit to the buyer's storehouse in the forei gn country. So the fact that there might be an antedated Bill of Lading would not, I believe, in this case affect the insurer's liability.

The second class of fraud relating to Bills of Lading is where the shipper obtains from the shipping company a clean Bill of Lading when in fact a claused Bill of Lading should have been issued. This happens in two circumstances. One, when the goods are shipped in a damaged condition and the damage is noted on the mate's receipt which is issued by the Chief Mate of the vessel acknowledging receipt of the goods, but the

remarks of the Chief Officer are not transferred to the Bill of Lading so that the Bill of Lading purports to show that the goods when received were in apparent good order and condition.

The second case in which a clean Bill of Lading is fraudulently issued is when the goods are shipped on deck. Generally, if goods are shipped on deck of a vessel, the fact that they have been so shipped must be stated in the Bill of Lading itself. If it is not stated on the face of the Bill of Lading, parties looking at the Bill will be led to believe that the goods have been shipped under deck in the holds.

In these two cases, the fraud operates against both the buyers and the insurers. In the first category, the insurers will face a claim from the buyers, when the goods finally arrive, for damage, and the buyers would probably produce the clean Bill of Lading saying : well the goods were in good condition when they were shipped, they arrived damaged, the damage must have occurred during transit, you insured this risk, please pay up. In the second case, except for the timber trade insurance, marine insurance policies usually contain a warranty that the goods are shipped under deck and therefore, by the shipper obtaining a Bill of Lading which does not state that the goods are in fac t shipped on deck, he is deceiving the insurers. In either of the above cases, if at the end of the voyage, a claim is made for damage, the insurer would be entitled to repudiate liability. However, it is the insurer who will be alleging fraud and he will have the onus of proving in the court that the terms of the policy were not complied with or that the goods were loaded on deck or that they were damaged at the time of shipment and this could be a very

difficult thing for him to do.

(3)
Another category of fraud in relation to cargo relates to the fraudulent jettison claims. These are particularly prevalent in the timber trade where cargo, as I said earlier, is commonly loaded on deck. What happens is that the shipper will, with the co-operation of the shipowner or his agent, obtain a Bill of Lading for a certain amount of cargo which is either not shipped at all or which is short-shipped. For example, the Bill of Lading may show 20 tons of timber as having been shipped when in fact only say 10 or 15 tons were actually loaded on board the vessel. During the course of the voyage, the vessel will encounter 'bad weather' as evidenced by the Log Book and for the safety of the ship and cargo, the non-existant cargo will be jettisoned and an entry to this effect will be made into the log book. Thereafter, the cargo owner will lodge a claim for the lost timber. In a case like this , apartfrom the obvious defence of a non-existant loss, the insurer will also be able to contend that as the goods insured and claimed for were never shipped, the policy never attached and the insurer was never at risk at all.

The above category of fraud ties in with the over valuation claims. These are cases where the insured cargo owner either obtains insurance for a greater amount of goods than are actually shipped or grossly over values the goods that have been shipped. It has been held that an over valuation of insured goods is a material particular that must be declared but how many cargo owners would you find who would go to the insurance company and say, 'I am shipping goods the value of which I declare is $10 million

but the real value is only $8 million'? But if the cargo owner does not
do that and the insurance company finds out that there has been such
an over evaluation, the insurer is entitled to repudiate the policy. There
are two grounds for this. First, on the ground of fraud, if the over
valuation was fraudulent or secondly, on the ground of non-disclosure
if the over valuation was innocently made but was a substantial over
valuation. In the case like this, the insured would not be able to recover
even the actual value of the goods lost. The whole policy would be avoided.

The fourth category of claims is that of the false shortage and damage
claims. In these cases, the insured, often with the connivance of the
surveyor appointed by the insurer, grossly exaggerates a claim he might
have for loss or damage to the goods during transit. This type of fraud
is generally committed by the consignee whereas the other cases discussed
earlier are mainly shipper frauds. In some cases, the insured is even able
to get the assistance of the shipowner's survey clerk. I have come across
one instance of this where working together the insured and the shipping
company's clerk inflated a large number of damage claims. The ultimate
loser in this case was the shipowner. For the insurance company having
settled the claims, looked to the shipowner for recompense based on the
survey report issued by the shipowner's own employee. Unfortunately,
by the time the fraud was discovered, the survey clerk had long since
left the shipping company and it was very difficult to get sufficient evidence
for prosecution. One of the things that led to this fraud being discovered
was that when the survey clerk resigned, he was rather careless. An employee
of the company, going through his desk later on to clear it up found that
in some cases, he had two survey reports for various surveys that he had
carried out : one showing the actual amount of the loss and the second

one showing the exaggerated amount of the loss which was used as the basis of the claim.

(3) Finally, of course, there is the claim which is fraudulent in all senses of the word, the claim in which from the beginning, no goods are shipped at all and in fact the goods never existed. In this case instead of goods, one in fact has only bits of paper which look authentic and purport to represent the goods. A claim of this nature is usually only found in cases where the ship supposedly carrying the goods has sunk in such deep water that all trace of the goods disappear and the investigators are unable to verify whether the goods were on board the ship at the time of the loss. However, there have been other instances of shippers selling non-existant cargoes and not shipping them at all and running away with the proceeds. A fraud of this nature, if it involves the shipowner and the vessel sinking, cannot be executed without the compliance of the shipowner and this leads us into the biggest area of marine insurance fraud, those involving the ship and cargo.

Hull fraud :

As far as the shipowner is concerned, there are two main ways in which he can defraud the marine insurance company and these two are interwined. They are scuttling and over valuation. Scuttling is the deliberate loss of the ship by the shipowner. It can be done in various ways : sinking the ship, setting it on fire, stranding the ship, damaging the machinery but the most popular way of losing the ship is to sink it deliberately. The beauty of the scuttling scheme is that the perils of sea faring are such that if one chooses the right time and the right place i.e place where it is impossible to recover or even inspect the sunken ship, the insurers

will have great difficulty in proving that the ship was deliberately cast
away though they may be very suspicious. Further, in order for scuttling
to be a defence to a claim for a sunken ship, the insurer must proved
that the ship was scuttled with the owner's consent. In fact, in the
Marine Insurance Act Section 55, subsection 2 provides that the insurer
is not liable for any loss attributable to the wilful misconduct of the
insured. Therefore, in proving that the sinking of a ship was due to a
scuttling, the insurance company must go further and not only show that
the ship was deliberately sunk by a member of the crew but that the owners
had a part to play in the sinking and there have been cases in which
the owners have been held entitled to recover under the policy because
the insurers were unable to show that they were involved in the scuttling.

Scuttling of ships has proved so profitable that there is now a major industry
of ship scuttlers operating. It has gone beyond the mere scuttling of the
ship and the industry now deals with fictitious cargo as well so that the
planners stand to recover not only the value of the ship but also the value
of cargo that was never on board. In some cases, in fact the main aim
of the conspirator is to defraud the cargo insurers and of the cargo buyers.
The scuttling of the ship itself is only a necessary incidental.

The most famous example of marine fraud on a large scale as operated
in Singapore is the case of the 'Glory Universe'. Many of you would be
familiar with this case from the accounts of the prosecution proceedings
in the newspaper. This was a universal fraud involving both the deliberate
sinking of a ship and claims for the value of fictitious cargo allegedly
on board at the time of the sinking. Two of the principles in the case,

Isaac Paul Ratnam and Ng Fook Khau have been tried and convicted on charges of conspiracy to cheat and attempts to cheat various insurance companies. The sums involved amount to more than US$10 million. This was a complex fraud which was operated in great detail. The conspirators obtained sales contract for the sale of various highly priced goods to buyers in Hongkong and Taiwan. These buyers then opened Letters of Credit in favour of the companies nominated by the conspirators. In addition, the conspirators prepared a large number of documents evidencing fictitious sales and thereafter, insured these fictitious goods with various insurance companies. The 'Glory Universe' was purchased by the conspirators and it was then purportedly loaded with cargo in Singapore pursuant to both the real and fictitious contracts in January 1979. The vessel left Singapore and after about six weeks, she sunk off the Pelawan Island in the Philippines. In the meantime, on the strength of false shipping documents including Bills of Lading, the conspirators negotiated the several Letters of Credit and obtained the proceeds thereof. In addition, after the vessel sunk, claims were lodged with the relevant insurers for the total loss of the cargo. The insurers were suspicious and started investigations which later led to the successful prosecution of Ratnam and Ng. The insurance claims were never paid. This was one case in which detailed investigation paid off for the insurance company.

The examples I have given above of the various types of marine frauds are all cases where if the insurers are able to prove fraud, they may vitiate the policy and be released from liability thereunder. There are however cases, where despite the fact that the insured matter has been

lost by fraud, the insurers rema in liable. These are cases in which the insured claiming under the policy are themselve innocent of any wrong doing and the loss arises from   a peril insured against.

The first category of such innocent insured comprises the mortgagees of vessels. It is usual nowadays for a bank or other company which is advancing money to a shipowner and taking as security for that loan, a mortgage over one or more ships, to require that not only the insurance policy over the ship be assigned to the bank but that the insurance policies be taken out in the joint names of the bank and the shipowner. In this way,the mortgagee bank becomes one of the named assured in the policy and has an original interest therein. If only an assignment of the insurance policy were taken, then the interest of the mortgagee in the policy would be derived from that of the shipowner and the mortgagee would stand in no better position vice versa the insurer than the shipowner. If sub-sequently the owner fraudulently sinks the ship, the owner's claim would be avoidable by the insurance policy on that ground. The mortgagee with an assignment of the policy is also tainted by the fraud of the shipowner and cannot recover. On the other hand, if the mortgagee is a named assured, he has an original interest in the policy and as long as he himself has not connived in or participate in the shipowner fraud, he can recover if he can show that the lost of the ship arose from one of the perils insured against. This is where the mortgagee has a difficulty because in most cases, the fraudulent shipowner gets rid of the ship by scuttling it. Scuttling in itself if not a peril which is insured against by insurance companies.

In one case, a valiant attempt was made to argue that a loss by scuttling lost by fraud, the insurer is retain... in simple... there are cases in which the named claiming under the policy are themselves... potential of showing

doing and the loss arises from ... a peril insured against.

The first category of sub-financing insured comprises the bottomry of records. It is not unknown for a bank or other company, which is advancing money to a shipowner, and taking as security for that loan a mortgage over the ship... effect not to rely on the insurance effected by the shipowner the ship be assigned to the bank but that the mortgage policies be taken out in the joint names of the bank and the shipowner. In this way, the mortgagee bank becomes one of the named assured in the policy and has an original interest therein. If only an assignment of the insurance policy were taken, then the interest of the mortgagee in the policy would be derived from that of the shipowner and the mortgagee would stand in no better position. Wherever the insurer finds the shipowner, if sub-... the owner fraudulently sinks the ship, the owner's claim would be avoidable by the insurer's policy on that ground. The mortgagee with an assignment of the policy is also tainted by the fraud of the shipowner and cannot recover. On the other hand, if the mortgagee is a named assured, he has an original interest in the policy and as long as he himself has not connived in or participated in the shipowner fraud, he can recover if he can show that the loss of the ship arose from one of the perils insured against. This is where the mortgage has a difficulty, because in most cases, the fraudulent shipowner gets rid of the ship by scuttling it, and this in itself is not a peril which is insured against by marine insurance companies.

In one case, a valiant attempt was made to argue that of loss by scuttling

in fact constituted a loss by perils of the sea. By a majority, the
House of Lord in England disagreed with this argument, holding that the
phrase 'perils of the sea' refers to fortuitous accident or casualty of the
sea and the word fortuitous itself involves an element of chance or
ill-luck.

A scuttling cannot be a peril of the sea because a scuttling is a situation
where those in charge of the vessel deliberately throw her away and there
is nothing fortuitous about this. In the case of the scuttling of the ship
therefore, the innocent mortgagee cannot recover. If however, the owner
sets fire to the ship and it becomes a total loss by reason of the fire,
the innocent mortgagee who is named in the insurance policy would be
able to recover because a loss by fire is one of the marine perils specifically
insured against. In fact, recently, my firm handled a case where a ship
was lost by fire. We acted for the shipowner against the insurer and another
firm represented the mortgagee bank. In that particular case, the defence
of the insurance company was that the ship had deliberately been set
afire by the crew under the instruction of the master. Now as I have
said this defence would operate against the shipowner but as in this
case, the mortgagee was innocent of any complicity in the plot, it did
not operate against them and the insurers, I think, recognised it because
they compromsied the case out of court.

The other category of persons who may be able to recover when there
has been a fraud are the innocent cargo owners. The most famous
example of a situation when innocent cargo owner has been held able
to recover under marine insurance policy is the Salem case. This involved

a very complicated conspiracy. A group of conspirators negotiated a multi-million US dollar contract for the sale of crude oil to a SOuth African company. To fulfill the contract, they purchased the vessel, South Sun, which they then renamed the Salem. The Salem was offered by the conspirators for a voyage to carry crude oil from the Persian Gulf to European and Caribbean ports. A company named Pontoil, an innocent company and a reputable trader, chartered the vessel and instructed the owners to send the vessel to Kuwait where it loaded about 2000 tons of crude oil. Pontoil then insured the cargo with Lloyds. After loading, the vessel was directed to Europe. As it proceeded on its voyage, the cargo was resold to Shell. The vessel sailed along the coast of East Africa and then instead of proceeding to Europe, it turned off and made for Durban in South Africa where almost all the oil was discharged. Thereafter, the vessel resumed her course and a few days later when it was off Senegal, it was deliberately flooded and abandoned by the master and crew acting on the instructions of the conspirators. The conspirators had in the meantime received payment from the South Africans of about US$50 million. The persons who were defrauded in this case were in fact Shell because they had paid Pontoil for cargo which never arrived. They were able to obtain some compensation, quite a substantial amount in fact, from the South Africans after the fraud was disclosed, but they later sued the insurers for the amount of their loss.

It was held that Shell were entitled to succeed on their claim. In this case, the goods had actually existed, so the policy attached at the time of loading of the goods. The fact that there was a scheme afloat to make away with the goods did not prevent the policy from coming on risk so

the question before the court was, was the loss due to a peril insured against. It was held by Mr Justice Mustill that there was here a loss caused by the peril 'takings at sea'. These words 'takings at sea' were held to cover a situation where the goods were lost through the deliberate acts of the crew committed at the instigation of the owner. "Taking" itself covered a wrongful misappropriation by a bailee and did not refer necessarily to a taking by somebody else who had not had possession of the goods originally. In this case, the 'taking' occurred when the ship left its direct course for Europe and made for Durban.

The important point to note from the cases that have been cited above is that even though a vessel or a cargo may be lost through fraud, an innocent insured can successfully claim against the insurance policy provided that he proves that the proximate cost of the loss was a peril insured against. I would therefore like to conclude my talk by saying that although a great deal has to be done in the detection of fraud and in the prevention of fraud, there are some cases where the insurers will find that they are still liable even though they have proved a fraud exists.

So, unfortunately, the insurer must recognise that in some situations, fraud is a risk which he has to take and if the fraud results in damage to an innocent party as long as the way in which the fraud was executed constituted a peril insured against, the insurer will have to be the person who bears the loss.

SHIP SCUTTLING

Speaker: Charles Haddon-Cave
Barrister-at-Law
London

SHIP SCUTTLING

(a paper read by Charles Haddon-Cave)

"Ship Scuttling" is defined in pleading terms as the "wilful casting away of a vessel with the connivance of her owners". It is referred to more colloquially as "rust-bucket fraud" or, more affectionately, by the aphorism "turn tappa" - which means, literally, "pulling the plug" in Greek.

Scuttling is a serious problem today. In recent years ships and their valuable cargoes have been disappearing in mysterious circumstances at an alarming rate, particularly in the Far East. Often, even though they strongly suspect fraud, underwriters have been able to obtain little or no evidence about the circumstances surrounding the loss and have been forced to pay up. The cost to Lloyds and the insurance market generally has run into millions of pounds each year. It seems that scuttling has become a very fashionable crime indeed.

History of "Scuttling"

Today's underwriter can , however, take some comfort from the fact that "scuttling" is not a modern invention. It had been popular long before Sir Francis Drake defeated the Spanish Armada or even before William the Conqueror crossed the Channel to beat the English.

Indeed, "ship scuttling" is as old as marine insurance itself. And you may be surprised to know that the concept of marine insurance has been traced back as far as 3000 B.C. to Chinese merchants who sailed up and down the Yangtze River.

The first recorded instance of the crime of scuttling is to be found in the works of the great Roman historian Livy who wrote in 215 B.C. about the merchants who were hired by Rome to transport much needed supplies to the Roman armies. He said, and I quote :

> "They either make false reports of
> shipwrecks which never occurred or they
> put a few things of trifling value on
> board old and shattered ships and when
> they have sunk them in the deep sea,
> the sailors escape in boats prepared
> for the occasion and then falsely tell
> stories that a great deal of merchandise
> was on board."

So, things have not changed - much!

You will have been told this morning by Captain Schulz about the practical steps that can and should be taken by hull and cargo underwriters to protect themselves against fraudulent owners. You will hear this afternoon from Captain Rivers, a member of the FERIT Investigation Team, about how marine fraud investigations are actually carried out. I am going to tell you about what approach the English Courts have taken in dealing with the problem of "ship scuttling" and what lessons there are to be learnt from past cases.

However vigilant the underwriting community is in dealing with disreputable ship or cargo owners and however thorough and painstaking an investigation into a suspicious loss of a vessel may be, underwriters must always bear in mind that at the end of the day, they may be sued in Court for non-payment of loss by an unscrupulous shipowner. It is important, therefore, for all concerned with the prevention and detection of this marine fraud to have an understanding of how the Courts approach such cases today. It is important for two reasons in particular. Firstly, so that they can have a better understanding of what evidence to look for and how to prepare the best case. Secondly, so that they will be in a better position to decide whether or not the ship or cargo owners' claim is one which underwriters have a good chance of successfully defending.

I shall deal first with two aspects of pre-trial procedure and how recent legal developments have swung against underwriters and in favour of shipowners. I shall then go on to discuss the burden of proof on the parties - what they have to prove and how far they have to prove it. Finally, I shall discuss what factors really influence the Court's mind and tell you about some of the more interesting, and sometimes amusing, cases that have come before the Courts in recent years. For instance, the case of the Master who rammed his ship up against a rocky shore, decided he had not done quite enough damage to cause a CTL, backed up his engines and rammed her again - all under the watchful eye of the local lighthouse keeper!

Two Aspects of Pre-Trial Procedure

The English Courts have always recognised the peculiar difficulties facing marine underwriters in scuttling cases; and for over 200 years marine underwriters have had two important procedural advantages over other litigants in the English Courts. However in recent years the pendulum has swung against underwriters and these advantages have been cut back.

Pleading "Particulars" of Scuttling

The first advantage was the fact that underwriters were not required to give "particulars" of scuttling in their Defence because usually such particulars were difficult to give. It was sufficient if they merely put the owners to proof of loss by insured perils and stated

that the vessel had been wilfully cast away with the connivance
of her owners. However, this practice has now been severely
modified by the Court of Appeal in two cases in 1972. Since
then underwriters have been required to plead the best particulars
of the allegations of scuttling that they can.[1] This
effectively means that underwriters are in no better position
than other defendants in non-marine fraud cases.

Order for ship's papers

The second advantage is what is called the "order for ship's
papers". This order goes well beyond the usual order for
discovery. It requires the owner to produce not only all relevant
documents in his own custody power or possession (for instance
log books, charts etc) but also to use his best endeavours to
obtain such documents from other sources (e.g cargo interests).
In the past it often proved to be an invaluable weapon against

(1) per Buckley L.J. in The Dias (1972) 1 Lloyds Rep. 187;

     see also The Gold Sky (1972) 1 Lloyds Rep. 331.

shipowners who tried to put up a "blank wall of silence". Until
recently an order for ship's papers was obtainable almost
automatically from the Courts. However, in 1972 the Court of
Appeal (2) decided that such an order should only be allowed as
a matter of discretion but that it should be granted where the
shipowner had been particularly "unco-operative" and "un-forthcoming"
with regard to the production of documents. The Courts will still,
however, in a proper case make an order for ship's papers before
the underwriters' defence is served and order a stay of proceedings

until the discovery is forthcoming. Since the decision requiring underwriters to plead particulars in their defence, it has become much more common for stays to be requested.

Assured's burden of proof

I now turn to the central question : the burden of proof. The burden of proof is perhaps the most important aspect of scuttling cases. As one well-known English judge said[2]:

(2) The Sageorge (1973) 2 Lloyds Rep. 521, see Lord Denning M.R.

"When ships and cargoes are scuttled ..... it is not easy for underwriters to probe or ascertain the truth. Their enquiries may sometimes run up against the blank wall of the dishonest who hope by silence to avoid detection .... (Usually) all the facts are within the knowledge of the assured, his servants or agents ....."

It is important therefore for underwriters to know exactly what they have to prove and how far they have to prove it.

In a case of scuttling that comes before the Courts the Plaintiff ship or cargo owners will be seeking to force the Defendants, the reluctant underwriters, to pay up for the total loss of his ship or cargo. So the initial burden of proof is on the Assured who must make out a prima facie case that the loss was caused by a "peril of the seas" or some other peril insured against. In order to establish, for example, a loss by "perils of the seas" the Assured must prove two things on the balance of probabilities : firstly, that the loss was caused by a "peril" that is to say,

something accidental or fortuitous; and, secondly, that it was caused by a peril "of" the seas, i.e. an accident connected with the sea and not merely something that could have taken place on land.[3]

Scuttling may be the "scourge" of the Maritime Community but it is not a "peril of the sea". Loss by scuttling, i.e. the direct and intentional admission of seawater, may be said to be "of the seas" but it is not a "peril" because the wilful act of the shipowner in procuring the loss deprives the catastrophe of the accidental character which is essential to constitute a peril of the sea.[4]

Section 55 (2) of the Marine Insurance Act 1906 expressly provides:

"The Insurer is not liable for any loss attributable to the wilful misconduct of the assured. But, unless the policy otherwise provides, he is liable for any loss proximately caused by a peril insured against,

(3) The Xantho (1887) 12 App. Cas. 509.

(4) per Collins L.J. In Trinder, Anderson & Co. v. Thames & Mersey Marine Ins. Co. (1898) 2 Q.B. 144 Samuel v. Dumas (1924) A.C. 431

even though the loss would not have happened but for the misconduct or negligence of the master or crew."

Where, however, the vessel is cast away without the connivance of the shipowner, that is the insured peril of "barratry" and the Assured can recover under the policy.[5]

I should first mention that because scuttling is not a peril of the seas even innocent cargo owners could not recover under marine policies. However, many policies nowadays (including those incorporating Institute Cargo Clauses F.P.A) have "seaworthiness admitted" clauses whereby insurers are bound to pay cargo-owners so long as they are not privy to the scuttling - which invariably it seems these days they are!

Incidentally, where a ship sails from her port of loading and is never heard of again the law raises a presumption that she has foundered at sea and the underwriters become liable for a loss by perils of the sea.[6] Section 58 of

(5) see e.g. Earle v. Rowcroft (1806) 8 East 135.

(6) Green v. Brown (1744) 2 Str. 1199

the Marine Insurance Act 1906 states :

> "Where the ship concerned in the adventure is
>
> missing, and after the lapse of a reasonable
>
> time no news of her is received, an actual
>
> total loss may be presumed."

Usually, however, some evidence does eventually come to the surface: crews are rescued, statements are taken, bits of wreckage examined, rumours begin to circulate.

Underwriters' burden of proof

Underwriters on the other hand normally have two strings to their bow. Firstly, they will merely put the Assured to proof that the loss of the ship was caused by perils insured against. So, if the Assured fails to convince the Court on a balance or probabilities that his story is true, he will fail against the underwriters. Secondly, underwriters will normally further positively allege that the vessel was scuttled, i.e. wilfully cast away with the connivance of the owners.

What do underwriters have to prove to succeed in an allegation of scuttling? They must overcome two hurdles : firstly, they must prove that the loss was caused by the deliberate and intentional act of someone on board the vessel, for example the wilful act of the Chief Engineer in causing an explosion or opening the sea inlet valves which was done with the intention of causing the vessel to become an actual total loss or a CTL. Secondly, underwriters must prove that the Assured procured the loss, for instance by hiring a "scuttling crew" to sink the ship.

The classic statement as to the parties' burdens of proof is to be found in the judgement of Mr Justice Brandon in The Gloria.[7]

> "The onus of proof that the loss was fortuitous
>
> lies upon the plaintiffs, but that does not mean
>
> they will fail if their evidence does not exclude
>
> all reasonable possibility that the ship was
>
> scuttled. Before that possibility is considered

some evidence in support of it must be forthcoming.
Scuttling is a crime, and the Court will not find
that it has been committed

(7) (1936) 54 Lloyd's Rep. 35, 50

unless it is proved with the same degree of certainty
as is required for the proof of a crime. If, however,
the evidence is such that the Court, giving full weight
to the consideration that scuttling is a crime, is not
satisfied that the ship was scuttled, but finds that
the probability that she was is equal to the probability
that her loss was fortuitous, the plaintiffs will
fail .... "

So, underwriters do not always have to prove "beyond reasonable
doubt" that the ship was scuttled. If they manage to produce the
same amount of evidence to show that the vessel probably was
scuttled as that produced by the Assured to show that the vessel
was lost by a peril insured against, it is the Assured who will
lose. Where the scales are equally balanced the Court will
simply find that the Assured has failed to discharge his burden of
proof. This happened in one of the most famous cases of recent
years The Gold Sky.[8] This ship sank 30 miles off Gibraltar about
10 years ago. The vessel's hull and machinery was insured against
the usual marine risks at Lloyds. The shipowners' story

(8) (1972) 2 Lloyd's Rep. 187

was that the vessel had suddenly developed a large vertical crack in the port side shell-plating of the engine room and the resulting jet of water had proved impossible to control and had caused the vessel to fill up with water and sink. The underwriters produced evidence firstly, that the thickness of the vessel's shell plating had been tested during a special survey immediately before the loss and was found to be satisfactory. Secondly, that the shipowners stood to gain financially from the loss. Thirdly, that the master and the infamous Third Engineer, a man called Komiseris whom I shall mention again later, deliberately tried to keep the salvors off the vessel. Mr. Justice Mocatta held that the Plaintiff shipowners had failed to prove, <u>on the balance of probabilities</u>, that the loss of the "Gold Sky" had been fortuitous; so their claim failed. However, the Judge went on to hold that the underwriters' evidence was not so strong that it justified a finding <u>beyond reasonable doubt</u> that the vessel had been scuttled.

A case in which the judge had no hesitation in finding scuttling was <u>The Tropaioforos.</u>[9] This vessel sank

(9) The Tropaioforos (1960) Lloyd's Rep. 569

in the Bay of Bengal on a flat calm morning in 1957 because of the incursion of seawater for 5 hours. The crew's story was that during the night they had heard a loud rumbling noise as the vessel struck "an unknown submerged object" and water began pouring

into the holds. Lifeboats were launched and boarded by the crew.
The radio officer remained on board to transmit SOS messages
giving a false position some 40 miles West of the true position
so that when help arrived the vessel had sunk without trace.
Unfortunately the officers, managed to drop all the log books
overboard having carefully packed their own belongings, as they
got into the lifeboats and the wireless operator was unable to
transmit from the lifeboat because he had accidentally transposed
the earth and aerial leads. The vessel was trading at a loss. It
was valued at £38,000 but insured for £200,000. In a judgement
running to some 30 pages Mr Justice Pearson held[10] that the
Plaintiffs had failed on a balance of probabilities to establish
that there was an accidental loss of the ship by perils of the
sea. Though it was strictly speaking unnecessary for the purposes
of deciding the case, the Judge went on to hold positively that
the ship had been scuttled. He said that there were just

(10)   The ~~Poole~~ Padre Island (1971) 2 Lloyd's Rep. 431; The Vainqueur

(1973) 2 Lloyd's Rep. 275.

too many "unfortunate" mistakes and too many "fortunate"
co-incidences.

Incidentally in two American scuttling cases recently reported in
Lloyd's Reports the United States Courts have adopted precisely
the same approach as that formulated by the English Courts.

What do the Courts look for?

What then do English and American judges look at when deciding whether or not a ship has been deliberately sunk? The best evidence is of course the ship itself which has usually disappeared without trace (often even without an oil trace!) Firm evidence is very hard to come by. Normally there is a carefully concocted and often quite elaborate story from the "rescued" crew about explosions and being in fear of their lives. Often only a few key members of the crew will be involved and it is rare for one of them to step forward and "spill the beans". The Courts therefore look, for instance, at inconsistencies in their statements and whether or not their story as to the manner in which the sinking occurred was technically feasible. In The Tropaioforos the Judge found that water could not have entered the engine room through a crack in the bulkhead because otherwise the engineers could not have failed to find the source of the leak. This, the Judge said destroyed the Plaintiffs' case. In fact, the Judge found, someone had pressed up all the tanks until they had burst and the bilge lines to the engine room were deliberately opened.

Sometimes the Court has an easier task in deciding whether or not a particular loss was deliberate, particularly where suspicious circumstances are coupled with extremely strange behaviour by the crew. There was the case of the Master who, with remarkable foresight ordered the ship's cook to prepare an especially

large breakfast for the crew in the early hours of the morning
of the casualty - presumably because he knew that they were in for
a very long day in the lifeboats! There was the case of the crew
who, with amazing foresight a few weeks before the fatal voyage,
conveniently booked hotel rooms at an obscure port off which
their vessel just happened to mysteriously explode and sink.

There was the case of the Broker who sent telexes to underwriters
saying that the vessel had sunk without trace and would they
please pay up when unfortunately her plimsol line was still
showing and she only sank two days later. On one occasion a number
of people went out to a ship which had grounded to see if they
could be of any assistance. As one of them started to climb up
the ship's ladder a crew member leaned over and shouted down :

"Get off! We don't need any help. If you come aboard we'll
cut your throats."

On another occasion an anonymous letter was addressed to Lloyd's
which predicted (accurately) that a certain ship would sink in
a few days - and she did! And in the case I mentioned earlier,
The Tropaioforos, when the crew were eventually rescued they
were found to be astonishingly well dressed and clean-shaven for
men who had hurriedly abandoned ship in the early hours of the
morning.

Connivance

If deliberate sinking is proved, then underwriters have a second
and often more difficult task and that is to prove the complicity
of the owners. As I have mentioned before, this allegation has a
higher burden of proof because it is essentially a criminal charge.
But it does seem that the Courts are much more prepared to draw
inferences from circumstancial evidence than they are in normal
criminal cases. This is particularly so when there is no evidence
of spite (or misplaced goodwill) on the part of the Master who has
sunk the vessel nor that he has any financial interest in throwing
her away. A judge explained lucidly how the Court's mind often
works :

> "Fraud must be brought home to a man with reasonable
> certainty. Suspicion, even though strong, is not
> enough. Such a finding blasts a man's character
> and may involve him in financial ruin.
>
> In enquiring whether there is something more which
> ought to change strong suspicion into reasonable
> certainty, it is obvious that one cannot expect to
> find direct evidence of connivance. Such expectation
> is precluded from the very terms of the enquiry.
> One can only look for facts, perhaps trivial in
> themselves, yet pointing in the same direction, as
> straws which show the way the stream flows; it may
> be the subsequent conduct of the owner, an expression

at an unguarded moment or an inference to be drawn

from something said or written which in other

circumstances would be innocent enough, but which

confirm suspicion when suspicion is aroused,

especially when the information so conveyed is un-

necessary for any legitimate purpose."

Those words were spoken by Mr. Justice Bailhache in 1922 in the

case of The Elias Issaias.[11] In this case the piece of

evidence that finally connived in the scuttling was a cable he

sent to the Master before the loss in which he quite unnecessarily

told the Master the amount for which the vessel was (over)

insured. This cable, the Judge said,

" .... was a strong hint for the Master that

the steamer was worth more to her owner at the

(11)   1922 13 Lloyd's Rep. 381, 386

bottom of the sea than on its surface."

The Elias Issaias was one of the dozen or so cases that came before

the English Courts immediately after the great shipping slump that

took place just after the First World War. All the ships were, as

a result of the slump, grossly over-insured and trading at a heavy

loss. Furthermore, their owners were in dire financial straights.

In the light of the cases such as these I have drawn up a checklist

of the kind of questions marine insurance investigators ought to have

in mind when they are investigating a shipowner in connection with a scuttling :

(1) Do the Master or crew have any personal incentive to sink the ship?

(2) Are there any unusual communications passing between the Master and the Owner?

(3) Does the loss look as if it must have been carefully planned with outside help?

(4) Is her owner financially solvent?

(5) Had he asked for advance freight?

(6) Is the vessel heavily over-insured?

(7) Is the vessel trading at a loss and a continual drain on her owner's resources?

(8) Had her owners been involved in other unexplained losses?

(9) Does they have any links with Cargo interests?

Finally, no discussion of shipowners' connivance in scuttling would be complete without a mention of the amazing case of The Michael.[12] In 1973 the "Michael" was on a voyage from the United States to Venezuela when she encountered heavy weather and her engines failed. A salvage tug came to her assistance and put a line on board. At about the same time it was noticed that her engine room was flooding and someone on the "Michael" cut the tow line. The crew panicked and abandoned

(12) The Michael (1979) 1 Lloyd's Rep. 55

ship and the vessel sank. The crew were rescued and taken

ashore at Curacao where a remarkable encounter took place. A
young English solicitor who had been involved in <u>The Gold Sky</u>
in 1968 was waiting to interview the crew of the "Michael" as
they came ashore. His own description of what he saw is set
out in Mr Justice Kerr's judgement :

> ".... as the tug was mooring, one of the crew members
>
> was heavily bearded and was looking at me in a
>
> curious way and I couldn't understand why and I
>
> couldn't place him: and when I looked back at him
>
> he was still looking at me and it suddenly dawned
>
> on me that he was none other than Komiseris (the
>
> man you may remember who scuttled the Gold Sky)
>
> (Q) Who spoke first? (A) He did and he raised
>
> his arms and eyes to the heavens and he said
>
> something like 'Oh no its impossible it can't be
>
> you' - rather as if 'Its a fair cop' was the look
>
> on his face .... "

With the infamous scuttler Komiseris found on board one could
be forgiven for thinking this was an 'open and shut case'.
However the owners pleaded barratry saying that the vessel had
been deliberately sunk by Komiseris who was acting alone without
their knowledge. The Judge believed the owners' story and found
in their favour - which just goes to show, ladies and gentlemen,
that one can't always predict what will happen in litigation!

SHIP SCUTTLING

DOCUMENTARY FRAUD

Speaker: Anthony Colman
Queen's Counsel
London

Introduction

In this talk I should like to discuss with you the extent
to which standard marine insurance policies on goods can protect
the goods owner against the kind of fraud which would involve
his never receiving the goods which he has paid for.

There are, I believe, two main problem areas.

First there is the kind of fraud which takes place before
even the goods are loaded on board the carrying vessel and often
depends upon bogus documentation. As we shall see, marine
insurance protection only has a very limited part to play in
this area. We are here concerned partly with the dishonesty of
the seller or shipper of the goods and partly with the dishonesty
of those who have the care of the goods at the port of shipment.

Secondly there is the kind of fraud which occurs once the
goods have been put on board the carrying vessel. I am thinking
about dishonest conversion or destruction of the cargo by the
shipowners themselves or under their instructions. That may or
may not involve fraudulent or bogus documentation. As we shall
see marine insurance is capable of providing a valuable protection
against this kind of loss, provided that you have the right kind
of cover.

Fraud before Loading

The first case is where the Shipper does not load the goods
expressed in the shipping documents and yet fraudulently presents
the shipping documents against the buyer's letter of credit and
obtains payment of the price of the goods which ought to have been

shipped. A similar case is where the shipper obtains bills of lading showing a shipment date earlier than that on which shipment was actually made in order to enable him to comply with a requirement in the letter of credit that there must be presented shipped on board bills of lading evidencing shipment by a date which has not been met.

In all these cases the purchaser of goods is likely to lose heavily due to the fraud of the shipper. The losses may be vast. The great Somali Sugar Fraud is a good example of how bad things can really be.

In 1974 the Somali Government through its purchasing organisation bought 10,000 metric tons of sugar from or through certain firms, some of which were, I am afraid to say, in Singapore, for a price of US$5.9 million C & F Berbera. It was a term of the contract that the buyers should open a letter of credit in favour of one of the Singapore firms for the full amount of the contract price. The Somalis duly opened their letter of credit for $5.9 million and it was as agreed confirmed by a Singapore bank. After some delay the Somalis were informed that the sugar had been shipped on the DELWIND from Koh Si Chang (Bangkok) and shipping documents, in particular bills of lading dated the 24th June 1974, were presented by the beneficiary under the letter of credit to the Singapore bank and the bank duly paid out US$5.9 million. When by mid-August the sugar had not arrived at Berbera the Somal is getting very concerned were told by a firm in Bangkok which said they were the agents for the Delwind that the vessel had broken down and that

they were sending two other vessels to off-load the sugar near
the Maldive Islands. One of the two other vessels, the Lord Byron,
eventually apparently cabled the Somalis saying that the Delwind
had only got as far as the Nicobar Islands and that transshipment
of the cargo into the Lord Byron was going slowly. Eventually on
10th October the Lord Byron docked in Berbera with not 10,000
metric tons of sugar on board but merely 687 tons of sugar on
board. It did however produce Mate's receipts indicating that the
sugar had been loaded from the Delwind at the Nicobar Islands.

You will not be surprised to hear that, first, on
24th June 1974, the date of the bills of lading, the Delwind was
not at Koh Si Chang at all. Worse than that, she had ceased to
exist, having been renamed earlier in June, and was on a voyage from
Yokohama to Portland, Oregon, and she never went anywhere near
Bangkok or the Nicobar Islands at any time during the period
June to October 1974. Moreover the sugar on the Lord Byron had
been put on board at Bangkok, not in the Nicobar Islands at all,
although the vessel had been chartered at the request of the
organisation which ought in the first place to have shipped the
10,000 tons of sugar on the Delwind. In these circumstances
it is perhaps not surprising that a whole proliferation of
litigation burst forth in the years following this disaster.
Indeed some of it is still alive to this day in the Singapore
Courts, but to my knowledge the Somalis have not so far succeeded
in recovering anything of the money which they paid out against
the bogus letters of credit in that case.

So what can the innocent buyer do when stricken by that
kind of disastrous fraud? Let me say at the outset that marine

DOCUMENTARY FRAUD

insurance simply does not set out to give protection against that kind of loss. No policy would ever have attached to the non-existent goods in the Somali case. In any event it is not part of the function of a marine policy on goods to protect the buyer against breaches of contract, however fraudulent, by the sellers or suppliers of the goods. The object of a marine policy is to protect the goods owners against loss or damage caused by accidents or fortuities occurring in the course of the insured adventure. What such policies do not do is to protect against losses caused by dealing with fraudulent sellers or shippers who set up an entirely bogus transaction for the purpose of milking the letter of credit. In such a case the unfortunate buyer of the goods is left to his remedies against the seller for breach of contract and fraud and return of the price and against all other parties who may have participated in the fraud his action will lie in the tort of deceit or conspiracy. He may also be able to trace the money into overseas bank accounts belonging to or controlled by the conspirators. But that remedy may be very difficult to pursue in practice because, first, the party who has been defrauded, as in the case of the Somalis, may not discover the fraud until weeks after the event, by which time the money may well have been effectively laundered beyond reach by the fraudulent parties. Secondly the fraudulent parties may have been able to dispose of the money into anonymous bank accounts in such places as Switzerland or to have paid it over to innocent recipients whose accounts are proof against tracing. Thirdly, the law as to tracing is complex enough in English law (see the decision of the English Court of Appeal in the extraordinary case of Banque Belge

v. Hambrouck (1921) 1 K.B. 321 where Bankes, Scrutton and Atkin L.JJ. all expressed quite different views as to the law of tracing and see also the discussion in The Law of Restitution by Goff & Jones, second edition at pages 48 to 60.) The problem of ascertaining the relevant principles of law in foreign jurisdictions is likely to create further delay which you will appreciate is very valuable to the fraudulent party in hiding the funds.

It may be that the defrauded party will have some remedy against the bank which issued the letter of credit or against the confirming bank for having made payment against documents which do not comply with the requirements of the letter of credit. Practically all letters of credit in international trade now incorporate the Uniform Customs and Practice for Documentary Credits (1974 Revision). These set out terms which are binding as between the banks and the party at whose request the letter of credit is opened and between the issuing bank and the confirming bank. I quote

> "ARTICLE 7
>
> Banks must examine all documents with reasonable care to ascertain that they appear on their face to be in accordance with the terms and conditions of the credit. Documents which appear on their face to be inconsistent with one another will be considered as not appearing on their face to be in accordance with the terms and conditions of the credit"
> "ARTICLE 8
>
> (a) In documentary credit operations all parties concerned deal in documents and not in goods.

(b) Payment, acceptance or negotiation against documents which appear on their face to be in accordance with the terms and conditions of a credit by a bank authorised to do so, binds the party giving the authorisation to take up the documents and reimburse the bank which has effected the payment, acceptance or negotiation."

"(c) If, upon receipt of the documents, the issuing bank considers that they appear on their face not to be in accordance with the terms and conditions of the letter of credit, that bank must determine, on the basis of the documents alone, whether to claim that payment, acceptance or negotiation was not effected in accordance with their terms and conditions of the credit."

"(d) The issuing bank shall have a reasonable time to examine the documents and to determine as above whether to make such a claim."

"ARTICLE 9

Banks assume no liability or responsibility for the form, sufficiency, accuracy, genuineness, falsification or legal effect of any documents or for the general and/or particular conditions stipulated in the documents or superimposed thereon; nor do they assume any liability or responsibility for the description, quantity, weight, quality, condition, packing, delivery, value or existence of the goods represented thereby, or for the good faith or acts and/or omissions, solvency, performance or standing of the consignor, the carriers or the insurers of the goods or any othe person whatsoever."

7

Actions against banks are difficult to pursue in practice because the defrauded party has the problem of showing that the bank should not have paid against the documents presented to it. In reality unless there is a clear lack of conformity with the documents as required by the letter of credit or there is some mutual inconsistency between the documents presented which really stands out so as to put the bank on inquiry under Article 7, the bank is entitled to pay and the defrauded party will have no recourse against it. What appears to be the most perfect set of shipping documents may, as in the case of the Somali Sugar Fraud, mask the most immense fraud. But unless the bank was put on enquiry, once payment has been made it is too late and the bank is not liable. The bank is under no duty to go behind the documents which on their face are in order and to investigate their authenticity, see Gian Singh v. Banque de l'Indochine (1974) 2 Lloyds Rep. 1.

The English Courts have leant over backwards to maintain the principle of the irrevocability of letters of credit and bank guarantees: see particularly the comments of Donaldson L.J. in The Bhoja Trader (1981) 2 Lloyds Rep. 256 at page 257 and I quote

> "In refusing to interfere with the sellers' right to call
> upon the bank to make payment under its guarantee, the
> learned Judge acted in conformity with the well-established
> principle that the court will not grant such an injunction
> unless fraud is involved ... . We agree with him.
> Irrevocable letters of credit and bank guarantees given in
> circumstances such that they are the equivalent of an
> irrevocable letter of credit have been said to be the life

blood of commerce. Thrombosis will occur if, unless fraud
is involved, the Courts intervene and thereby disturb the
mercantile practice of treating rights thereunder as being
the equivalent of cash in hand.".

Buf if the party who has opened the letter of credit discovers
before presentation of the documents or before payment under the
letter of credit that a fraud is to be committed or that documents
are forged, the courts will order the bank not to pay if there
are sufficiently strong indicia of fraud: see the recent decision
of the English Court of Appeal in United City Merchants v. Royal
Bank of Canada (1981) 1 Lloyd's Rep. 604.

Indeed, the bank has a duty not to pay, however perfect the
documents may seem, if it has evidence of fraud or forgery. In
practice the bank may be placed in a very awkward position because
it may have great suspicions as to the honesty of the beneficiary
but the evidence of fraud or forgery before it may be very marginal
and if it were ill-founded and the bank failed to pay it would be
liable to the beneficiary. It remains for the courts to work
out with greater clarity how strong the evidence has got to be before
the bank can refuse to pay. In Edward Owen v. Barclays Bank (1981)
Q.B. 159, Geoffrey Lcne L.J. as he then was, said at page 175E that
the only circumstances which would justify a bank in refusing to
pay would be "if it had been clear and obvious to the bank" that
the party in question had been guilty of fraud. Stephenson L.J.
in the United City Merchants case referred to above at page 623
says that the banker must not pay if he knows that the bill of
lading, in that case, is a forgery or false. It may be an
interesting matter for discussion later on at this Seminar,

particularly amongst those of you who are bankers, how strong the evidence ought to be before payment is refused.

Finally all merchants who suffer loss in this way should perhaps hesitate a little before they adopt the remedy tried by the Somali Government. It promptly seized the Lord Byron and the Master and the crew. The Master was imprisoned for a very long time and the vessel was kept under arrest for so long that her owners abandoned her to the underwriters as a constructive total loss, which I believe was ultimately accepted. Perhaps, though, this remedy will not be in the power of 'most defrauded buyers.

Theft or deprivation of the Goods at the Port of Shipment before Loading

The scene that I have in mind is the arrival of the goods at the port of discharge in crates or packages which are quite in order to all outward appearances but are found on opening to be filled not with goods which the receivers have purchased but with old scrap and rubbish. The goods have of course already been paid for by means of a letter of credit. It is usually not very difficult for the ship to prove that this substitution could not have been perpetrated on board. So it is either a fraud perpetrated by or with the connivance of the shipper or the work of thieves operating in the country of shipment or at the port of shipment.

If the shipper is responsible, the principle is the same as in the cases of non-shipment which I have already mentioned. The receivers' remedy is against the shipper or the seller for breach of contract or fraud. There is no claim under the marine insurance policy on the goods. If the shipper is not responsible

the receiver may be able to recover from the insurers of the goods. Under the old traditional Lloyds SG Policy which is set out in the First Schedule to the English Marine Insurance Act 1906 goods are insured only from the time when they are loaded on board the carrying vessel. Nowadays goods are normally insured under the Institute Cargo Clauses (F.P.A.) or (W.A.) or under the Institute Cargo Clauses (All Risks). In the case of each of these extensions of cover there is a Transit Clause in the following form:

"This insurance attaches from the time the goods leave the warehouse or place of storage at the place named in the policy for the commencement of the transit, continues during the ordinary course of transit and terminates either on delivery

(a) to the consignees' or other final warehouse or place of storage at the destination named in the policy

(b) to any other warehouse or place of storage, whether prior to or at the destination named in the policy, which the Assured elect to use either

(i) for storage other than in the ordinary course of transit or

(ii) for allocation or distribution, or

(c) on the expiration of sixty days after the completion of discharge overside of the goods hereby insured from the overseas vessel at the final port of discharge,

whichever shall first occur."

Where the goods have been purchased on CIF terms the buyer of the goods will become assignee of the contracts contained in the policies on the goods and he can therefore claim on the policies in respect of loss of the goods before shipment, provided that the loss

occurs within the ambit of the transit clause (i.e. after leaving the warehouse at the port of lading) and is caused by an insured peril.

Unfortunately owing to a very odd feature of the English law of marine insurance, the Lloyd's Standard SG Policy reference to "thieves" does not cover clandestine theft but involves violent theft only: see Rule 9 of the Rules of Construction. In La Fabrique de Produits Chimiques v. Large (1922) 13 Ll.L. Rep. 269 Bailhache J. voiced doubts as to whether in a warehouse to warehouse (transit) clause policy the element of violence was necessary. But this point has never been finally decided. However, many policies now incorporate the Instutute Theft and Pilferage Clause in these terms and I quote.

> "It is hereby agreed that this Policy covers the risk of Theft and/or Pilferage irrespective of percentage. No liability for loss to attach hereto unless notice of survey has been given to Underwriters' agents within ten days of the expiry of risk under the policy. Underwriters to be entitled to any amount recovered from the Carriers or others in respect of such losses (less cost of recovery if any) up to the amount paid by them in respect of the loss."

This clearly would cover wrongful substitution of rubbish for the contents of crates and packages even in the absence of any violence.. If the All Risks Clauses are incorporated the problem does not arise: they cover all losses caused by any kind of fortuitous event.

A further difficulty may arise where the receiver has purchased the goods on FOB or C & F terms rather than CIF terms

and takes out his own policy on the goods. It is trite law that the C & F or FOB buyer acquires title to the goods as from the time when the bills of lading to shipper's order are negotiated and he assumes the risk of loss or damage as from the moment of shipment on board the vessel. If the theft occurred before shipment how can the buyer have an insurable interest in the goods when they were stolen at a time when the risk remained in the shipper? How can the policy attach to goods which were never shipped, which were therefore not the subject matter of the bills of lading and in which title never actually passed to the insured buyer? Is he left in the position where although the goods were stolen within the scope of the transit clause and although the seller has negotiated the letter of credit and been paid the price, the buyer has no remedy against his underwriters? The point is still open but I do not believe that this is the position. The solution is provided by section 6(1) of the Marine Insurance Act. I quote

> "The assured must be interested in the subject-matter
> insured at the time of the loss though he need not be
> interested when the insurance is effected:
> Provided that where the subject-matter is insured, 'lost
> or not lost', the assured may recover although he may not
> have acquired his interest until after the loss unless at
> the time of effecting the contract of insurance the assured
> was aware of the loss and the insurer was not."

The effect is that the assured is <u>deemed</u> to have had an insurable interest at the time when the loss occurred and, one has to interpolate, provided that the loss occurred within the ambit of the transit as defined by the transit clause. I believe that one

is entitled to treat the insurable interest as notionally
arising before risk would have passed to the buyer under the
sale contract had the goods been shipped in the first place.
It must, however, be accepted that this is a very cloudy area
of marine insurance law.

Conversion of the Goods by the Shipowners

No account of modern marine fraud could possibly be
complete withoutreference to what may aptly be described as
the Mahler's Eighth Symphony of marine fraud - the amazing case
of The Salem (1981) 2 Lloyd's Rep. 316.

The facts are utterly astonishing and I can only give you a
brief outline here.

The conspirators obtained a contract with a South African
organisation under which they agreed to sell Middle East oil to
it and deliver at Durban for a price of about U.S.$50 million.
Against the security of that contract they obtained a loan from
a South African bank sufficiently large to pay for the purchase of
an oil tanker - no mere coaster, but a 200,000 ton super-tanker!
The price was U.S.$12.3 million. The conspirators manned the
tanker with a master and crew who were prepared to co-operate
with the conspirators in their plan. The conspirators then put
the tanker up for charter for oil cargoes from the Gulf to Europe
and duly fixed the vessel to an innocent charterer for carriage of
a full cargo from Kuwait to Europe. The vessel then loaded the
cargo and all documents issued to the shippers provided for
carriage to Italy. The vessel then proceeded on the voyage and
having changed her name from Salem to Lema she diverted to Durban
where she duly discharged as much of the cargo as her pumping

arrangements allowed. The buyers of the cargo thereupon paid the purchase price, all of which disappeared into Swiss bank accounts except that which had to be paid to the South Africʌn bank in repayment of the loan to purchase the tanker. After discharging all but 15,000 tons the tanker left Durban and followed the usual course to Europe, the conspirators sending from time to time as she went various messages designed to show that the voyage to Europe was proceeding normally. Two weeks after leaving Durban, while off Senegal, the vessel was scuttled on the orders of the conspirators and she sank with the remainder of the cargo: the object being to conceal evidence of the fraud. By the time the receivers realised what had happened the oil discharged at Durban had been refined or irretrievably commingled with other oil and the purchase price of the oil paid by the South Africans had disappeared into Switzerland.

So it was the shipowners themselves who were responsible for this staggering loss. In this case the sellers of the oil did get paid for it by the buyers and the ultimate buyers, Shell, took up and paid for the documents after the loss was known, as they were obliged to do under their purchase contract. Every document they got was a perfectly genuine document in one sense. But although the bills of lading did represent a real contract of carriage from the Gulf to Europe, that was a contract which the shipowners from the outset had no intention of performing. The ultimate owners of the cargo - Shell - brought an action to recover their loss from issues were referred to the Commercial Court in London. I emphasise that the All Risks clauses were not incorporated. All would have been much simpler if they had been.

15

The first question was whether this was a loss by barratry. Mustill J. rejected this contention on the grounds that you cannot have barratry unless the acts of the crew were directed **against** the shipowners and as the real shipowners were the conspirators themselves and as the charterers could not be treated as the shipowners a necessary prerequisite of barratry was absent.

The second question was whether the loss was caused by persons acting maliciously. Mustill J. also rejected this contention. The Court of Appeal had held in 1969 in The Mandarin Star (1969) 2 Q.B. 449 that this peril covered losses caused by spite of ill-will and this was not the case with the Salem. There was no personal malice against the cargo owners.

The third question was whether this was a "taking at sea". Mustill J. held that it was. Wrongful misappropriation by a bailee in the course of the voyage clearly fell within that peril. The taking occurred when the shipowners did an act vis-a-vis the goods which constituted a deliberate disregard of the obligations owed under the bailment by the charterers, namely when the vessel turned off course to Durban. Accordingly the loss was caused by an insured peril.

In recent years there have been a number of instances of allegations that shipowners have converted goods to their own use in this way and the decision makes it clear that in most of such cases the policy will protect the cargo owner, there having been a taking at sea.

Where the shipowners scuttle the ship with cargo on board, there will normally be a loss by perils of the sea under the Institute FPA Clauses. This is due to the effect of the second

part of clause 8 of the Institute Clauses. This clause provides and I quote:

> "In the event of loss the Assured's right of recovery
> hereunder shall not be prejudiced by the fact that the
> loss may have been attributable to the wrongful act or
> misconduct of the shipowners or their servants, committed
> without the privity of the Assured."

This provision was originally introduced primarily to enable mortgagees to recover in respect of vessels which the owners had caused to be scuttled and where the assured mortagee was innocent of fraud: see Samuel v. Dumas (1924) A.C. 431 and other cases in which it was held that a loss by scuttling was not an accident or fortuity of the adventure and could not therefore be covered by the Lloyd's SG form. One of the consequences of this principle was that an innocent cargo owner whose goods had gone to the bottom with a scuttled hill could not recover, for at that time the Institute All Risks Clauses had not been introduced. The effect of clause 8 is that if the ship sank with the cargo on board due to its having been deliberately cast away with the knowledge of the assured one can treat the loss as caused by perils of the sea, that is to say it is deemed to have occurred without the wrongful act or misconduct of the shipowners or their servants. By this curiously round-about way the innocent cargo owner can recover for the loss of his goods. Needless to say, if he is a party to the fraud his claim will fail.

Where the All Risks Clauses apply this problem does not arise because they automatically cover loss of the goods by whatever cause, provided that it is not caused by delay by inherent vice or by the wilful misconduct of the assured.

17

Conclusion.

In this paper I have tried to outline the kind of cover which the goods owner obtains from the standard London forms of policy in cases where there is a fraud affecting goods. I hope it will be appreciated from what I have said that the buyer of goods from overseas is best protected if he has the benefit not of the ordinary marine policy with the Institute Cargo Clauses (FPA) but of the All Risks Clauses. The latter are, of course, more expensive than the former. Of course, the cargo owner is even further protected if he can satisfy himself as to the honesty of his seller and of the primary shipper because against their dishonesty and fraud a marine policy is not designed to offer him protection.

MARINE FRAUD AND ITS PREVENTION

Speaker: Capt P J Rivers
Thomas Howell Kiewit (S)
Pte Ltd
Singapore

MARINE FRAUD AND ITS PREVENTION

A "devil's triangle" - ships losses, insured perils -
unseaworthiness - substandard ships - rise in losses in
this area - FERIT. The syndicate theory - ordinary
enquiries into losses - FERIT's review of losses 1959 to
1979 - a pattern emerged - a number of scuttlings strongly
probable - Pattern of 'Rust Bucket' frauds - other reasons
for scuttling - Charter Party Frauds which can also include
scuttling and theft "Documentary" frauds, false Bills of
Lading etc - consignees not insurers foot the bill for
these and misdescribed or (generally) substituted goods -
'Non-Delivery' frauds - parties involved - detection -
necessity to pool information on all losses - how the
system aids the criminal - Police investigations and
limitations - prosecutions "JAL SEA CONDOR", "TIEN PAO",
"TONGA" & "GLORY UNIVERSE". Prevention - Insurers - Bankers -
Documentation-Certificates of Survey - Bills of Lading -
Register of signatories - Control of shipping agents and
shipping companies - shareholders - failings of some authorities - the International Maritime Bureau.

MARINE FRAUD AND ITS PREVENTION

There was in early 1981 an article in the newspaper suggesting
that there might be a "devils triangle" in the South China Sea
because of the mysterious disappearance of a number of ships.
The thought may have been inspired by the well publicised
"Bermuda Triangle" theory. But these "unexplained" losses have
another explanation.

Ships of course have been sinking ever since they were first
built. Historically, fire has probably been the worst enemy of
any well found ships especially if wooden built. With the intro-
duction of steam, collisions were to cause losses while vessels
stranded because of faulty navigation or by striking uncharted
rocks and so on.

These and other casualties including storms and piracy were
recognised hazards and when marine insurance developed in recent
historical times they could be grouped together under the
heading of "insured perils".

But while heavy weather might overwhelm an unfortunate vessel,
what of the craft which foundered in calm seas? Was it because the
vessel was rotten or was it something more sinister?

In the former case, the vessel would have been unseaworthy. That
is not in a fit and proper state to undertake the contemplated
voyage. Thanks to the legal fraternity unseaworthiness which
did not necessarily mean unsafe came to have an ever widening
interpretation. In fact, it is now almost impossible for any
ship to be absolutely seaworthy in the legal sense.

A new word has now come into fashion "substandard". This has
been applied to vessels registered in countries which may not
enforce international connections regarding manning and seaworthiness. Generally too this has been applied (but not
exclusively) to Flags of Convenence countries (F.O.C), Liberia,
Panama, Honduras, Cyprus and even Singapore. Some of whom

maintain high standards and some who don't. In any event, substandard ships came to mean usually overage vessels under poor management, badly maintained, poorly equipped with under or unqualified officers and indifferent crews.

In recent years, there was in this area an alarming rise in marine losses which may have been due to substandard vessels but some of which were not satisfactorily explained or indeed not explained at all.

As a result, insurers in Hongkong, Singapore and Malaysia with of course interested underwriters of Lloyds of London, set up their own, if the term could be used, Commission of Enquiry. Based in Hongkong, it was called the Far East Regional Investigation Team or FERIT for short. Their task was not primarily to conduct investigations but to review the many losses which had occurred and to distinguish those which may not have been genuine or which could not be accounted for by the operation of an insured peril. They were particularly interested in looking into a theory advocated by some that there was a 'syndicate' at work which was scuttling (i.e deliberately sinking) ships for money.

It should be explained that normally, when an insurance claim is made, a surveyor is appointed to assess the extent of damage and briefly report the circumstances so that the insurers could decide if a claim is payable under a policy. In the event of a total loss such as the ship sinking, both hull and the various cargo underwriters would appoint their own surveyors. For fear of cargo claims, the shipowner would be advised by their P & I Club (the insurers for cargo liability) and their lawyers to say as little as possible. To claim for their hull insurance, however, rather more details would be supplied. Many surveyors although capable technical men would possibly accept what they were told on its face value. Few made any attempt to connect different losses. The reports supplied to the several insurers would thus vary in detail and quality while the information was rarely shared

amongst the various insurers.

FERIT began to look into those losses which firstly occurred in the period 1978/9 and then back as far as 1959. They eventually short-listed 48 vessels from which a pattern emerged. Most of these vessels were over 15 years old under 3000 tons gross and flew the Panamanian flag. Surprisingly, only three of these ships were known not to have been classed (a vessel is said to be classed when it has been subjected to a survey by a classification society such as Lloyd's Register). However, the report noted that the percentage of these vessels under the (Japanese) NK Class was 52.6. They elsewhere noted that only three of the vessels lost were registered in Japan.

A sub-standard vessel would obviously fit within this pattern so a further look was required to see where the money was - that is, was hull or cargo over-insured or were values at risk excessive or any other anomaly eg. was there an undue amount of high valued goods in a low valued ship.

Some of the losses could be eliminated but in the end, 27 of the 48 losses considered were highly suspect or thought strongly probable of having occurred as the result of scuttling. Further-more, common names of crew members, ship owners agents, and cargo interests were uncovered so that it could be said "that not only have a number of different small syndicates operated, but also there has been a passing on from one party to another of the latest 'techniques'".

This then was the overall picture in this region which included sinkings not only in the South China Sea but in the Indian Ocean as well. But within this framework, there were a variety of different frauds.

The ones involving the highest values were the 'rust bucket' type. An old ship with a low insured value of say US$250/300,000 would go down supposedly carrying high valued cargo. Electronic goods figured in most manifests (the total values of goods would vary

from S$2 million to almost S$30 million on different ships).

A leak from an unknown cause would occur in a hold and in some unexplainable manner the engine room would then flood. The radio would be (possibly intermittently) unserviceable and the crew would take to the boats without loss of life and be rescued within hours by a passing ship who would give a position miles away from where the Master reported his vessel to have gone down (which incidentally was invariably in the deepest water on the route). The weather was always calm when the vessel was abandoned although storms were said to have been encountered just before. Sometimes the vessel just disappeared. In one case, a few years ago, the whereabouts of a vessel which left Hongkong for Singapore was only discovered when it was reported that she had been in a collision in Kaoshiung. At that time, she was being towed to be broken up!

Although a number of different names for the consignees and shippers might appear on the Manifest, enquiry would show that they were connected. Bills of Lading would be without Letterheads or be different from the purported carriers. Names of the ships or shipping companies often resembled more respectable ones, while the ships were often 'singletons' (i.e in a one ship company) and had been newly purchased.

A variant was to scuttle a ship after stealing valuable cargo such as consignments of tin ingots. This may have been done without the knowledge of the owners (in which case it would be barratry) but not very often.

Other reasons for scuttling would be to hide the fact that inferior goods had been shipped. In one instance, with genuine cargo under some 250 bills of lading, a ship was sunk because there were four consignments of grossly over insured goods on board.

Charter Party Frauds form another type. In their simpler form, a charterer pays the first month's hire, puts the ship on the berth

to load "freight prepaid" cargo and absconds with the proceeds.
The next month, the shipowner quite naturally wants his money
and the cargo interests just as naturally dont't want to pay any
further freight. At one time, there were some 15 to 20 ships
held up in various ports (mostly obscure) around the Indian Ocean
with large and valuable amounts of timber destined for the
Middle East.

Charter Party Frauds normally do not involve scuttling but one
shipowner, it is believed, tried to justify the legal abandon-
ment of the voyage by setting fire to his engine room. When this
did not work, several attempts were made to sink or burn the
ship before success was achieved.

Theft on a large scale will sometime motivate the charterer.
For example, a charterer will order the ship to Singapore and
there discharge the entire cargo, say, of rubber for transhipment. The ship will then sail off and the charterer will sell the
cargo.

Others have found the above frauds too cumbersome. With 'rust
buckets', too many parties have to be involved while stolen goods
have to be disposed of. It is much easier to sell non-existent
goods shipped on vessels which either do not exist or are in some
other part of the world. These are generally termed "Documentary
Frauds" and are aimed at innocent consignees rather than at
insurers. A genuine policy may be presented to the Bank but if
there were no goods, the risk never attached and it would be void.

This type requires a sale against a genuine Letter of Credit, a
false Bill of Lading with false invoices and packing lists. A
false surveyors certificate might also be included. A variant
is to have a genuine surveyors certificate of goods sighted at a
warehouses but never shipped.

It should be noted that banks cannot be held responsible if the
documents presented are not genuine.

It is of course not uncommon for a seller to misdescribe the quality or condition of his merchandise. But with certain high value goods, a buyer has received drums of water rather than say patchouli oil or black sand instead of valuable minerals.

These instances of substituted goods often occur after surveyors have sighted the real commodities in a warehouse away from the port area.

Another fraud aimed at insurers is the 'Non-Delivery' type. Cases of 'something' are shipped on a genuine and respectable carrier usually to places where the ports are not well regulated. The cases have been genuine labels fixed above false addresses. At the discharge port, an accomplice removes the label. A non-delivery certificate enables the consignee to collect on his insurance and the cases, usually containing junk, are left to moulder as unclaimed cargo.

A variant is to send genuine goods and later put a different address on top and with the connivance of the port clerical staff, have it transhipped to another port.

Shipping companies staff may become involved. For example, valuable machinery may not be collected by the consignee who obtains a 'non-delivery' certificate. After payment by the insurer, the accomplice issues a Delivery Order and splits the proceeds. The insurers of course are never informed of the discovery.

These are just some of the frauds that man can devise. There are many more.

In most of the cases outlined above except for theft or Charter Party Frauds, the shipper would rarely be an innocent party. 'Rust Buckets' required the connivance of the shipowner or his manager. These might also involve consignees where Letters of Credit facilities are required. Consignees could also be involved in 'Non-Delivery' frauds.

Detection of the fraud may come about during the investigations following a notice of the loss of the ship or the long overdue

arrival or non-delivery of the goods (inferior or substituted goods would of course be detected after delivery). There have, however, been cases where insurers have been alerted by circulars from their associations or by the receipt of anonymous warnings.

In some instance, at least photographs were taken of a vessel prior to sailing which showed that some of the goods were not on board.

The spate of scuttlings in this area managed to run for such a long time for two main reasons. Surveyors enquiring into their particular loss who might be admirable in the normal course of their duties did not investigate fully and therefore issued reports which did not indicate anything untoward. Or because information was not pooled, a pattern did not emerge.

Where the fraud is aimed at insurers, the system aids the criminals because of the outlook of some lawyers and insurers. Some popular beliefs are quoted as follows : 'insurers are not policemen' (from an insurer), 'the cargo underwriters accepted the premium so they should pay the claim' (from the lawyer for a P & I Club) and 'oh well never mind the premiums can be increased to include an element for fraudulent claims' (from an insurer).

Furthermore, surveyors are limited in their powers to investigate while the Police who have the authority may not be able to act because the crime (e.g scuttling) may have occurred outside their jurisdiction.

Even when they do investigate a crime, a very high standard of proof is required. In Hongkong recently, the owner of the "JAL SEA CONDOR" was brought to trial mainly on the evidence of the Master & Chief Engineer. But their testimony was discounted when it came out they had been promised a reward by the insurers.

In places where English law does not apply, it may be that convictions can be obtained. In Taiwan, some crew members and some cargo interests involved in two different losses like the "TIEN PAO" and the "TONGA" were sent to prison for scuttling.

In Singapore, a different approach was tried in the S$23 million fraud involved in the loss of the "GLORY UNIVERSE". A long and thorough investigation carried out by the Commercial Crime Division enabled the Attorney General's Office to present such a strong case that after a lengthy trial, an accused changed his plea to guilty on four charges with another 38 to be taken into consideration. He was sentenced to 11 years in prison but scuttling was not among the charges which included conspiracy and the use of false shipping documents.

It was to the latter charge that earlier two other gentlemen pleaded guilty and were sent to prison for up to six years. They were involved in three ships including the "GLORY UNIVERSE".

But often, the Police cannot start an investigation because no report is made to them. Complainants may be in another country. Insurers have even been advised not to make a report as it might be construed as an admission of liability. Also insurers wish to preserve a good public image or do not want to admit to bad experience.

The question of prevention must be considered. The simple answer is that the merchant (for the frauds all batten on their activities) should exercise more common sense and suppress greed. Most marine frauds are perpetrated by con men who in every field have offered something at an attractive price with perhaps shady overtones. Shipowners are offered a good hire rate for their vessels. Shippers are quoted a below average freight rate to ports which are not properly serviced and charter party frauds develop. Goods are quoted at below market rates or they may be difficult to obtain through the usual channels and another documentary fraud is possible. Even with the rust buckets, the otherwise honest shippers have been drawn in because "the insurance will pay".

Publicity also helps to deter these practices. Even before FERIT was formed, the journalists of the Far Eastern Economic Preview

produced a number of particularly good articles which brought the spotlight of publicity to bear.

Since the FERIT report insurers have become more critical in their acceptances of risks, it would be presumptuous to comment further except to suggest that some losses should not be left to ordinary surveyors no matter how competent they might be in their normal work. And although insurers prefer to pay up for commercial reasons and shun the publicity, it might be better to face a court action rather than settle a suspect claim.

Banks should develop a more critical attitude towards the clearance of documents rather than rely on Article 9 of the Uniform Customs & Practice for Documentary Credit which says that Banks assume no liability or responsibility for genuineness or falsification of any documents. After all, they carry out checks of their own before making loans.

The merchant himself should see that the documentation is as thorough as possible with independent checks. Mr Eric Ellen, the former Commissioner of the Port of London Authority Police has pointed out that one buyer requested ten different documents which as it turned out all came from the same source. One gentleman from Taiwan even issued his own Certificate to say that goods existed in Singapore.

A Certificate of Quality issued by the most reputable of surveyors is not sufficient if the goods were sighted at a warehouse at a distance from the loading berth. A follow-up Loading Survey ensures that the goods are not substituted and indeed that they are shipped.

This suggestion is however deprecated by some of the most reputable of shippers because it may take place after the loading date specified in the Letter of Credit which can usually be avoided by obtaining a predated bill of lading.

This matter of predated Bills of Lading indulged in for commercial reasons by respectable shipowners & merchants alike is a practice

which lends itself to fraud.

Indeed, it is amazing how casually Bills of Lading are handled as they are the keystone to so many frauds. Banks have accepted Bills of Lading with Letterheads or titles of shipping companies which are completely divorced from the vessel named and may even be non-existent. Indeed Bills of Lading without any names printed on them have been passed.

It has been suggested that the number of persons authorised to sign Bills of Lading be limited, that Master should countersign them and that a register of signatories be maintained and supplied to Banks.

Consignees buying CIF should be most careful in specifying which ships should carry their goods as should any shipper. To use vessels operated by a well-known liner service or handled by established agents is one thing but for others, some form of rudimentary check should be carried out.

It has been suggested in Singapore that a register be kept in the Marine Department giving not only the details of the agents but their principles as well. The licensing of agents and brokers of ships might help.

Ownership of vessels is often difficult to establish. Changes of owner from one front company to another is not unknown. Recently, the Singapore Government announced that an enquiry was being made into the affairs of one Singapore Group which flagrantly abused the ease of transfer permitted in Panama. It has been suggested that an international register be kept.

Considerable criticism of Flags of Convenence have been made because there is no check on standards. Indeed, of the many Panamanian losses which have occurred, none have been investigated by any Marine Authority least of all the Panamanians. Harbour officials have rarely checked beyond the face value of certificates presented

to them. Although manifests are supposed to be given to the
Authorities, this has not always been done and they are not
available to surveyors who generally have to provide sufficient
information before the Police can start their investigations.

Dissemination of information is of course essential. There is
Lloyd's Register but their agents around the world cannot always
obtain the requisite information. The FERIT Data Bank will be
available to insurers but what of the others?

At the beginning of 1981 under the auspices of the International
Chambers of Commerce (based in Paris), an International Maritime
Bureau was set up under a recognised fraud expert, Mr Eric Ellen,
who is mentioned earlier. The IMB is expected to supply information and to carry out enquiries even before a business transaction is agreed. This should be most helpful provided that not
only are its services utilized but that other bodies and individuals
provide a feed back of information.

Finally, no matter what safeguards are devised, someone will find
a way around them. The rfraud merchants have found accomplices
in the insurance industry, bankers have become involved in
disreputable transactions, classification societies have not maintained
standards, surveyors have issued fraudulent certificates and respectable shipping agencies have inadvertently accepted doubtful ships.
It sounds hopeless but why make it easy for the criminal?
Prevention is naturally better than cure.

MARINE INSURANCE CLAIMS AND SHIPS OWNERS' LIABILITY

Speaker: N K Pillai
Advocate & Solicitor
Singapore

MARINE INSURANCE CLAIMS AND SHIPOWNERS' LIABILITY
BY MR N K PILLAI

The subject of my lecture is of paramount interest not only to
Underwriters but also to shipowners. Cargo claims, as they are
commonly referred to, form an integral part of every marine
Underwriter's overall view of marine risks. Quite a considerable
part of a marine insurer's time and expense is devoted solely to
cargo recoveries. In Singapore, cargo subrogation recoveries are
an invaluable source of 'return income' to insurance companies.
It is also in subrogation recovery actions that insurers learn
some useful underwriting conditions and make the necessary adjust-
ments. From the shipowners's point of view, these cargo claims are
often construed as a constant 'nuisance' and indeed a very considerable time and expense is spent in dealing with these claims. The
cargo claimants at all times try to present the best case possible
and the shipowners likewise try to put up the best defence possible.
It is the main theme of my lecture this morning.

My attempt is only to provide a bird's eye view of the legal
aspects, the practical aspects and the technical aspects involved
in cargo claims. As such and by necessity, the notes are brief in
content. To many of you, whatever is to be said, would be confirm-
ation of your own practice over the years, but to some, it would
serve as a useful telescope to view and deal with the ever urgent
marine cargo claims.

The written words on the subject are numerous and if one is to
give a comprehensive lecture, we would all be here till dark.

More so, lawyers tend to be verbose whereas claims managers and others in similar positions want crisp answers.

THE CONTRACT OF CARRIAGE

It is incumbent upon the cargo owner to show that the shipowner is either in breach of his contract of carriage and/or has been negligent in his care and custody of the goods. In order to do this he must have the evidence to demonstrate how the damage and/ or loss to his cargo was occasioned and then examine the contract of carriage to see if the shipowner is liable.

A bill of lading serves three purposes. It is a receipt given by a shipowner in acknowledgement of the shipment of the goods specified in the bill; it is a document of title to those goods; and it may also be evidence of the terms of the contract of carriage under which the goods are to be carried and delivered by the shipowner.

Where a bill of lading is in the hands of the charterer of the vessel, the goods are carried on the terms of the charter party. Subject to this, however, in most cases, the bill of lading will take effect as a contract between the holder of that bill and the shipowner. This is primarily due to the fact that most bills are signed for and on behalf of the Master and/or contain a demise clause or "identity of carrier" clause expressly identifying the owner of the ship as the relevant carrier and party to the contract. This however is qualified in two respects :

(a)   in containerised transport where door-to-door bills are issued by freight forwarders or container operators, the operative contract of carriage may be with either of these parties;

(b)   charterers' names appearing on the bills - under Singapore law and English law not affected, if bill signed for and on behalf of master with expenses or implied authority or contains a demise clause. The charterer is not liable and their name is a mere decoration.

The safe course may be to protect the position against both.

Liability under a bill of lading is governed in the majority of the cases by the Hagne Rules or the Hagne-Visby Rules incorporated either expressly by the terms of the bill of lading or by force of law if there is legislation at the part of shipment expressly requiring the same. On the first score there is usually little problem. By operation of law, it is meant that the country of the port of shipment where the bill of lading is issued may have legislation enacted by its legislature providing that outward shipments are to be subject to the Rules and the bill of lading must say so.

Under the Hagne Rules, the shipowner is liable for loss or damage occasioned to the cargo in transit unless the carrier can demonstrate the exercise of due diligence before the commencement of the voyage to make the vessel seaworthy and cannot avail himself within one of the excepted perils. The Rules also prohibit strictly any attempt

to deviate or lessen liability by carriers as being repugnant. Thus, if you come across any attempt at shortening the time bar period from the established Hagne Rules period of one year and/or reducing in limitation figures, you can complain of such attempts as being contrary to the spirit of the Hagne Rules.

A bill of lading may either acknowledge that goods have been shipped or that goods have been "received for shipment". A "shipped" bill is used where whole cargoes have been delivered and taken aboard. A "received for shipment" bill is used where there are parcels of cargo lying on the wharf to be placed on the ship. Art. VII of the Carriage of Goods by Sea Act 1924 and Section I of the Bill of Lading Act 1855 explain the use of "received for shipment" bill.

When the shipper delivers the goods at the place of loading he is given a Mate's Receipt unless there is a custom at the port to the contrary. If the goods are damaged this fact should be distinctly noted on the face of the receipt. Wherever possible, Masters of vessels should arrange for goods to be tallied as they are delivered to the ship. Thus, it is normal in cases of shortages, to request for such shipment tallies. A bill of lading must be accurate as to the quantity and as to the condition of the goods and it must also be correctly dated.

Where there is a statement as to the amount shipped being qualified

by such words as "weight unknown", the bill of lading is not even prima facie evidence against the shipowner of the actual amount shipped. Where a bill of lading states that the weight and description of the goods and elsewhere contain the words "weight, contents and value unknown", the statement of weight and description are taken as having been made by the shipper and not verified by the person who signs and issues the bills. Where there is erroneous description of the goods, the shipowner will always be liable. The effect of the words "weight, contents and value unknown" is to in some way make the contract one for the carriage of the package, whatever its contents. Art. III Rule 3 of the Carriage of Goods by Sea Act 1924 imposes upon the shipowner a duty to declare the quantity or weight or number of packages or pieces as furnished by the shipper unless he has reasonable grounds for suspecting that the shipper's figures are not accurate or unless he has no reasonable means of checking them. A statement in the bill of lading which is qualified by the words "said to weigh" and others alike does not prevent a shipowner from proving the true facts since by making that statement he is deemed to be repeating merely what was repeated to him by the shipper, see NEW CHINESE CASE ENTIMONY COMPANY v OCEAN STEAMSHIP CO.

One of the principal considerations for all cargo claimants is Time-Bar. The Hagne be brought within one year of final discharge of the goods. Under Singapore law, following English law, a writ

.. 6/-

must be issued within the one year period and no enlargement of time can be given by the Court. However, normally, time extensions are given by shipowners and their P & I Clubs. But it is important that in these cases the time extensions are obtained from the correct parties and in writing. If the time to file a suit falls on a Sunday and/or a Public Holiday, under Singapore law, one is allowed to file it on the next working day. By virtue of the Gold Clause Agreement, parties to same have a two year time limit. In all cases, my own experience has shown that Underwriters are always inevitably pressed within this rule as sometimes settlement of the claims themselves take a very long period, especially involving shipments to the Middle-East, Africa and South-America. It is very important that Underwriters when instructing Solicitors give full available details concerning the claims so as to obliviate the necessity to seek further instructions urgently under pressure. Some of the important details are :

(a) bill of lading number and date;

(b) description of cargo in the bill of lading;

(c) amount damaged and/or short-delivered;

(d) c.i.f./f.o.b. sale;

(e) addresses of shippers and consignees and their
     corporate status;

(f) if transhipment involved, similar details and where
     transhipped and name of vessel; and

(g)   where known port of registry of vessel is.

This will enable Solicitors who are instructed in the eleventh-hour to file suit properly.

The Hagne Rules stipulate that "in any event" the shipowner should not be liable for an amount exceeding £100 sterling gold value per package. In the United States of course, much litigation is afoot to evolve a jurisdical definition of what really is a package and the American Courts, with respect, are well ahead in the proper course. A problem quite different in nature and susceptible to the global economic situation is the value of "gold". One school is of the view that the Hagne Rules meant £100 sterling whereas another school contends that the present day value has to be properly established for the amount of gold worth £100 in 1924 which currently may be in advance of £8000 sterling. Under the Hagne-Visby Rules however, the figure is £400.

Apart from the per package limitation, shipowners can also limit in England, by virtue of Section 503 of Merchant Shipping Act 1894 to a maximum currently of £35.93 per ton (S.I. 1980 No. 1872) of their vessel's net registered tonnage together with the addition of engine room space. In Singapore, the corresponding enactment is found in S. 294 of the Singapore Merchant Shipping Act(Chapter 172) and the amount per ton is S$206.60. However, by S.295 of the same Act, limitation will not be available where it can be shown that the loss had occurred with actual fault and privity of the owner - see the interesting case of "LADY GWENDOLEN" (1965) 1 LL.R. 355.

JURISDICTION

The next hurdle for a cargo claimant is the issue of jurisdiction. If the contract of carriage contains an express jurisdiction clause, then that jurisdiction should be considered. But sometimes it is impossible to serve or bring the shipowner within the jurisdiction under the bill of lading and as a result, proceedings are commenced elsewhere. In Singapore, whenever proceedings are commenced within this jurisdiction under a bill of lading which has express reference to another jurisdiction, the shipowner is entitled to and always inevitably seeks a stay of proceedings. Generally, if the shipowner can show that the claim is more closely connected with the other jurisdiction and is more convenient in relation to the availability of witnesses, then he will be entitled to stay, although he would be usually ordered to appear in the other jurisdiction and if the time-bar limitation had operated, not to plead it as a defence. Two interesting authorities on this issue are "EL AMRIA" (1981) 2 LLOYDS 119 and AMERCO TIMBERS PTE LTD v CHATSWORTH TIMBER CORPORATION PTE LTD (1977) 2 MLJ 181.

Sometimes in the case of bulk shipments, the governing voyage charter party is incorporated in the bill of lading by for example, "all terms and conditions of the governing charter party". Although this does not bring in an arbitration clause but where the bill of lading expressly states that the arbitration clause is

deemed to be included, if proceedings are commenced, shipowners can apply for a stay.

DAMAGE TO CARGO AND CLAIM

The cargo claimant can only recover from the shipowner for damage to cargo occasioned whilst the same was under his care and custody. For this the cargo claimant must prove that the goods were loaded on board the vessel in good order and condition and discharged damaged.

Whenever there is any visible damage to cargo upon loading, the Master is expected to endorse this on the face of the bill of lading. If he fails to do so, the shipowner will be estopped from denial. The issuanceof a clean bill of lading in these circumstances is clearly contrary to established law. However, the damage must be apparent on reasonable inspection to the Master so that hidden damage is not covered - see SILVER v OCEAN STEAMSHIP CO (1929) AER 611. All preshipment damages must be referred to shippers or suppliers and recourse may be had under Common Law as under the Sale of Goods Act. It may be opportune moment here to bring to your notice the pernicious practice of persuading ship-owners to issue clean bills of lading against Letters of Indemnity. If the goods are visibly damaged, this practice tantamounts to a fraud upon third party endorsees of the bill and the fraud had been perpetrated by the shipowner and the shipper in concert. In such a circumstance, the Courts may refuse to enforce the Letter of Indemnity in the event where the Shipowner is subsequently held

liable, see the decision in BROWN JENKINSON V PERCY DALTON (1957) 2 AER 844.

Damage to cargo after discharge must always be properly surveyed and noted. Every possible step should be taken to ensure that all the available evidence on this is gathered and in this respect I recommend some guidelines :

(a)   a good surveyor should be appointed;

(b)   the surveyor should set out his findings in a manner that omits no details and that will as a rule permit the Underwriters to make their decision on the claim;

(c)   claimants should be reminded of their duty to apply to the claim agent at the port of discharge for a survey without delay;

(d)   the claimant should be reminded of his obligation to file notice of claim with the ocean carrier and/or other third party concerned with the loss without delay;

(e)   the survey should be held promptly - in many commodities contamination can spread swiftly and immediate steps are necessary to keep damages to a minimum;

(f)   carriers representatives and/or third party representatives should be invited in writing for a joint survey and if this invitation is declined, this fact should be recorded in the report;

(g)   cargo manifest and storage plans should be cripped for and

obtained, where necessary;

(h) where chemical analysis is necessary, this should be attended to; and

(i) where the surveyor is unfamiliar with the commodity, prompt steps should be taken to consult an expert who has the necessary knowledge to express an authoritative opinion on the cause and extent of the damage.

An invaluable advice is on claims procedure itself and I advise the following :-

(a) notice should be given to Underwriters or agents promptly in writing;

(b) surveyors with experience should be appointed and instructed to report to you at the first available opportunity;

(c) where the claim is large and not straight forward and/or if doubts or queries are raised in your minds or you are put on a self-enquiry, consult solicitors who can outline investigations and advise you properly so that your rights are protected;

(d) shippers and/or consignees must be reminded that they must act as if uninsured and take all reasonable steps to minimize and/or avert the loss or damage;

(e) clean receipts should not be given where damage clearly visible;

(f) documents required to support a total loss claim;
   - the original and all negotiable copies of the policy of insurance duly assigned to the claimants;

- the shippers' invoice and if applicable packing list;

- complete set of bills of lading duly endorsed;

- when necessary the Masters' protest;

- copy of notice of claim filed with the ocean carriers or other parties responsible;

- ship's agent at discharge port should be advised of all payments of total loss claims;

- letter from carrier confirming full shipment on board at time of loss;

(g) documents required to support a particular loss of particular average claim :

- evidence of insurance as above;

- the shippers' invoice and if applicable the packing list;

- copy of bill of lading;

- surveyor's report or other authentic document confirming the loss or damage and giving details of the extent of the loss;

- evidence of the condition of the goods on discharge;

- copies of notice of claim on carriers and/or third parties with their replies (if any) ;

- accounts for any cargo sold;

- accounts for any extra charges incurred;

- statement of claim from the claimants;

- Master Notice of Protest in some cases;

- loading survey in certain cases;

SECURITY

This is extremely vital in relation to enforcement of judgements.
The usual method is a bank guarantee or a P & I Club guarantee.
The best possible method is of course to arrest the vessel. In
Singapore, the claimant has to swear an affidavit by his
solicitor demonstrating a strong prima facie case against the
shipowner and that the requirements under the Administration of
Justice Act are satisfied. Qualification of the security required
is to add the claim amount to the interest rate for the number of
years it would take for trial to that of costs. In England,
another useful method is by way of the "Marera" injunction, which
is also allowed in Singapore under Section 4 of the Civil Law Act.
By this method, where proceedings here have already been commenced,
if the Defendants attempt to remove the assets from within the
jurisdiction so as to defeat judgement, the Court will allow the
injunction restraining the Defendant from doing so.

An important point to note is that where proceedings have been
commenced, a right of arrest will still survive even if vessel
is sold subsequently to third-parties - see the "MONICA S".
But, if proceedings have not been commenced before the sale of
the vessel, then an arrest will not be possible thereafter.

STATEMENT OF CLAIM/SUBROGATION

Cargo claimants would have to show that they have "title to sue"
and their financial loss. Before doing this, the process of

subrogation must be completed.

DAMAGE BY COLLISION

Where damage to cargo is caused by the collision of two or more ships, in many cases, it will not be possible to recover from the carrying ship while the offending ship can be sued for under the tort of negligence but only to the extent of that other ship's fault or blame in the collision.

LITIGATION

One of the crucial aspects of marine insurance practice for insurers is litigation. This can be principally in two areas;
(a)   liability under the contract of insurance; and/or
(b)   recovery against party (ies) responsible for loss or damage.

In this complex process of litigation, three basic issues should be borne in mind and instructions addressed to them :
(a)   the strength and weaknesses of your case;
(b)   the length of time that would take; and
(c)   the costs.
As such, your instructions to solicitors at the outset must contain :
(a)   a detailed synopsis of the facts of your case -
      here you must outline - if it is an issue of liability
      under the policy - the various aspects of the Marine
      Insurance Act as related to the facts so that your
      Solicitors can advice you on the law relating to them;
      and

(b) all available evidence.

Your instructions must end by requesting (usually) the following :

(a) advice on the legal position;

(b) advice on the evidence - further investigations, if any;

(c) procedural advantages, if any; and

(d) advice generally.

A bad advice is always the result of bad or poor instructions. It is in the realm of evidence that your assistance is most needed. You are the best source on issues of fact. Before consultation or conferences with your solicitors, you must master your facts.

In cases of defence under the contract of insurance, you must specifically request if you solicitors are "happy" with the available evidence or should further investigation be carried out so that all available avenues have been explored. They should also be asked what procedural steps can be taken to "flush" out evidence from the claimants, gain advantages into the case and generally weaken the cases as a whole. It is always good tactics to investigate and have the available evidence in hand before the Defence is filed. In this way, you will be able to apply for Further and Better Particulars of the Statement of Claim and generally map out the weak points in the plaintiff's case. If your solicitors are not fully confident of the success of the defence, their

advice must be obtained as to what percentage should be admitted and a payment made into Court so as to take advantage of costs. It is a good rule of the thumb that in complex cases, your solicitors are aquainted with the matter from inception so that, in fact, they can guide you and/or your investigators as to the nature of the evidence generally needed for a successful defence of the matter.

In cases of claims in recovery, much of the rules outlined above will apply with an additional one being that your solicitors should be asked for periodical status reports until the case has been set-down for trial. In such cases, time is of the essence; if the claim is a substantial one, a large potential "income" is pending. It is therefore essential that Claims Managers aquaint themselves with basic knowledge of the types of pleadings in recovery cases and the time span governing them under the Rules. It is recommended that all claims of US$25,000 and above be scheduled as follows :

Name of Action	File No.	Date Writ Filed	Date Statement of Claim	Date Reply	Date Summons

Success in defence or in claims is not entirely dependent upon the ability of your solicitors or Counsel but to a large extent on the support and direction given by you. A good and knowledgeable client is half the battle won in litigation.

====

A CASE STUDY FROM HONGKONG

Speaker: Paul Bugden
Solicitor of Supreme Court,
UK & Hongkong
Hongkong

A CASE STUDY OF MARINE FRAUD IN HONGKONG

BY PAUL BUGDEN

I am asked to deal today with a case study of Marine Fraud in
Hongkong. I should say at the outset that, by its vary nature,
marine fraud is seldom, if ever, restricted in its perpetration
to one jurisdiction. Indeed, if this were the case marine fraud
might not present such a formidable problem as it does today.
In truth, whilst the series of frauds which I have chosen for
portrayal have numerous connections with Hong Kong, a number of
other jurisdictions are inevitably involved.

Broadly speaking, the frauds which I shall be examining are of
the documentary variety. I am asked to adopt an illustrative
approach rather than an analytical one and I believe that there
may be some advantages in doing so. I hope that in approaching
the subject by way of an illustration, I will have drawn out some
of the elements in this case study which are common to many other
instances of fraud of this type. In doing so, I hope that some
of the pitfalls will be highlighted and that perhaps as a result
they will be avoided more often in future.

The events I am about to discuss were revealed in the course of
enquiries initiated by insurers of various consignments of cargo
which proved never to have existed. During the investigations
into the shipment a picture emerged over a period of some two
months of a series of frauds perpetrated by the same group of
people. Inevitably, investigations concentrated on those features

which were of interest to clients and therefore some areas of the picture were never clearly in focus. I will recount the events historically and I apologise for any apparent lack of detail in certain areas.

It was probably in about April of the year in which these frauds occurred, that a vessel, suitable for their purposes, was located by the conspirators, languishing in a port in Taiwan. She was a general cargo vessel of the Panamanian registry with a G.R.T a little over 3,700 tons and was 25 years of age. She had holes in her weather deck and cracks and holes in her shell plating. Her special survey was due within the next six months and experts subsequently expressed the view that it was inconcievable that she could have passed that survey. Accordingly, I shall refer to her as the good ship "RUST BUCKET".

Two of the conspirators offered to pay the previous owners of this good ship US$240,000 in cash. The vendors must have been very impressed with this offer as the vessel's scrap value was subsequently estimated at only US$160,000 just two thirds of the proposed purchase price. One assumes that it was in their eagerness to accept this favourable price that the vendors also, rather foolishly, agreed to leave half the purchase price outstanding and secured only by way of a mortgage on the vessel.

Having acquired the vessel, it is believed that the conspirators

set about defrauding a Hong Kong bank of US$1 million. This
aspect of the matter is one of the blurred parts of my picture.
Apparently the good ship "RUST BUCKET" had been purchased by a
Panamanian company which I shall call A. This company was
controlled by the conspirators.   It is believed that the vessel
may have been registered by company A under a name other than
the good ship "RUST BUCKET" by which she came to be known during
the course of the events I am relating. It is believed that the
conspirators managed to obtain a fraudulent valuation certificate,
possibly in Indonesia, showing the vessel's value in excess of
US$1 million. In other words, four times the figure they had
actually agreed to pay. Armed with this false valuation certificate
the conspirators proceeded to Hongkong as the directors of a second
Panamanian company B. They approached the bank in question and
requested a loan of US$1 million to assist in the purchase of the
good ship "RUST BUCKET".   The bank were persuaded to lend this
sum on the strength of the false valuation certificate and the
loan, like the second part of the purchase price, was secured by
way of a mortgage on the vessel.

The formalities were completed and the purchase price was paid
by the conspirators, in their role as directors of Panamanian
company B, to themselves, as directors of Panamanian company A.
The bank duly registered their mortgage against company B and
the good ship "RUST BUCKET" in Panama on July 16th.

Having acquired the vessel for a down payment of only US$120,000 and having acquired what transpired to be a permanent loan of US$1 million the conspirators had a reasonably heathly balance in their favour with which to finance the remainder of their schemes. Essential to their plans was the establishment of an international trading company and a shipping agency in Hong Kong. This proved to be an easy task.

On May 13th, in the year of our fraud, a business was registered in Hong Kong with a grandiose English name. I shall call it the Trans Global Trading Corporation. In reality this was nothing more than a sole proprietorship run by a Fukienese gentleman, who was one of the leading conspirators. The Business Registry was provided with a false residential address for this gentleman, who it is thought may not have been permanently resident in Hong Kong at this time. He rented a small office and employed a staff of two. Having paid a small deposit and one month's rent and installed a telephone our Fukienese friend was in business.

Two days later a limited company which had lain dormant for four years but had previously been a shipping and general trading company was reactivated. The company had had two Hong Kong Chinese as directors. One of these resigned and was replaced by a Thai gentleman. The Thai and the remaining Cantonese were also central figures in these frauds. Again, this company acquired small business premises, which were comprised of only two rooms and

once again only one month's rent had been paid in advance. In keeping with Trans Global Trading Corporation the residential addresses, as provided by the directors in the public records, were false. For the purposes of this case study, I shall call this company Slick Operators Ltd.

At this time, the good ship "RUST BUCKET" was in Hong Kong. It is not known how she got there from Taiwan or what had happened to those who had sailed in her. The conspirators had a little time on their hands, during which they decided the vessel should be in gainful employment. Panamanian company B appointed Slick Operators Ltd as agents for the vessel in Hong Kong. Slick Operators Ltd then fixed the vessel to carry steel from Korea to Iran.

The next step was to equip the good ship "RUST BUCKET" with a new crew. As luck would have it our Thai friend had connections with two other agencies in Hong Kong, both of dubious repute, whose business involved crewing. Slick Operators Ltd appointed one of these companies as their agents for crewing matters only. These agents found a Cantonese Master, who I shall call Skip, and a crew in the Kam Lung Tea House, a well known haunt for seaman in Hong Kong. The formalities required by the Seaman's Recruiting Office were completed by Slick Operators newly appointed crewing agency and the crew were mustered on July 12th. They were paid one month's wages in advance.

Captain Skip was ordered to sail from Hong Kong in ballast bound for Inchon to load the cargo of steel.

Meanwhile, our Fukienese friend of Trans Global Trading Corporation fame had been busily securing purchase orders from various Singaporean importers for consignments of car air conditioners and high density polythene. The proposed sales by Trans Global Trading Corporation were on C and F terms and payment for these consignments was to be under Letters of Credit. As you will know the seller obtains prompt payment under a Letter of Credit by presenting to an advising bank in his own country those documents specified in the body of the Letter. These Letters of Credit required only that the advising bank in Hong Kong be presented with copies of signed invoices and packing lists and full sets of "on board", "freight prepaid" Bills of Lading endorsed in blank and naming the appropriate notify party. These three categories of documents could, of course, all be prepared by Global Trading Corporation or their friends at Slick Operators Ltd. But more of this later.

On July 27th, in the year of these frauds, the vessel arrived at Inchon. Our Cantonese friend from Slick Operators Ltd arrived on board with a fixture note, which indicated that Slick Operators Ltd had fixed the good ship "RUST BUCKET" to load five thousand five hundred metric tons of angle iron and carry it to Khorramshar, Iran. As Captain Skip had observed water entering the vessel's holds

through a leak in the port side of No. 1 hold and into holds 2,
3 and 4 through the holes in the deck, he advised our Cantonese
friend that the vessel could not possibly sail to Khorramshar.
Whereupon Captain Skip was successfully pressurised into agreeing
to take the cargo to Hong Kong where, he was told, it would be
transhipped to destination.

As it happened, the vessel was not capable of loading the full
cargo and following a little patching up she sailed from Inchon
on August 6th loaded to her Plimsol Line with something in the
region of four thousand seven hundred metric tons of iron angle
bar having shut out to the balance of eight hundred metric tons.

The angle iron had been purchased by five consignees in Khorramshar
on C and F terms for US$1.2 million, which was paid under Letters
of Credit. They were destined never to see their cargo. Slick
Operators Ltd received US$150,000 in return for their freight prepaid
Bills of Lading.

On the journey to Hong Kong a typhoon was reported and Captain Skip
having no doubt taken all factors into account wisely decided that
his good ship should shelter in Keelung. After two days, she put to
sea and arrived in Hong Kong on August 17th.

Once the vessel had berthed our Cantonese friend arrived on board.
He instructed the Master to discharge the cargo so it could be
reshipped to the Middle East. He indicated that the vessel would

be going to Taiwan for repairs which was no doubt a matter of some relief to Captain Skip and his crew.

It will come as no surprise that subsequent enquiries revealed that, following discharge, our Fukienese friend sold the angle iron. He found purchasers in both Singapore and Indonesia and concluded sales with them in the name of a trading company bearing his own name as its title. The cargo was allegedly reshipped in three different vessels, one of which could be traced to have arrived at Singapore with 2,170 metric tons of angle bar. Exactly what happened to the remainder of the angle bar is not known. It may even have been sold a second time in Hong Kong.

Shortly after the vessel had concluded discharge, Slick Operators Ltd prepared a number of Bills of Lading showing that various consignments of car air conditioners and high density polythene had been shipped on board the vessel by Trans Global Trading Corporation. These Bills of Lading were dated August 21st and were stamped 'freight prepaid'. They showed various Singaporean importers as the notify party and were signed by our Thai friend at Slick Operators Ltd. As required by the Letters of Credit, the Bills of Lading were subsequently endorsed in blank by Trans Global Trading Corporation. At about this time, it may be assumed that the staff of Trans Global Trading Corporation were busy preparing invoices and package lists for these cargoes.

Needless to say no cargo was actually loaded. Having completed all the formalities required by the Letters of Credit our Fukienese friend presented them to the advising bank in Hong Kong and received payment of a sum in the region of US$3 million.

On August 22nd the good ship "RUST BUCKET" was cleared for Manila. However, Slick Operators Ltd ordered Captain Skip to sail in ballast for Kaohsiung, Taiwan for repairs. This piece of subterfuge was no doubt intended to delay enquiries.

The vessel arrived in Kaohsiung on August 26th, but no repairs were commenced as no funds had been provided to her agents there.

At about this time Trans Global Trading Corporation vacated their offices leaving the rent unpaid. On September 8th , our Fukienese friend also vacated his residential premises. Shortly thereafter Slick Operators Ltd also decamped paying no rent.

To add insult to injury on September 22nd the good ship "RUST BUCKET" broke loose from her moorings and collided with another vessel. Had this incident not occurred and been reported in Lloyd's Casualty Reports it might have taken investigators considerably longer to unravel these events, as the whereabouts of the vessel would have probably remained a mystery for a considerable period of time.

This series of events left behind a motley collection of creditors. It included the following :-

A CASE STUDY FROM HONGKONG

1. The vendors of the good ship "RUST BUCKET" who were looking for the balance of the purchase money amounting to US$120,000. They, along with some of the other creditors, arrested the vessel.

2. The Hong Kong bank which had parted with US$1 million on the strength of a mortgage on the vessel.

3. The disappointed Iranian consignees of the angle iron and their underwriters, who were still wondering why their cargo had not arrived.

4. The crew who were a little short on salary and repatriation expenses. They also arrested the vessel.

5. Various importers in Singapore and their finance houses who had paid for the car air conditioners and high density polythene and were also wondering why their cargoes had not arrived.

6. The landlords of the offices of Trans Global Trading Corporation and Slick Operators Ltd.

There were probably also a host of bunker suppliers, repairers, stevedores, chandlers, ship's agents and other minor creditors who were also reflecting on their misfortunes.

Having outlined the story of these frauds, I would like to reflect upon the reasons why the conspirators were able to succeed. I believe that there are two factors of particular significance. Firstly, the ease with which individuals can establish companies and businesses and commence trading in certain jurisdictions and

secondly the failure of those with whom the conspirators dealt
to make proper enquiries into their bona fides.

I believe the first factor is capable of some improvement. The
demands of the modern commercial world are such that individuals
should be free to form companies and businesses with the minimum
of government supervision or interference. It is easy to
anticipate that any suggestion of closer Government regulation
of company and business formation and operation would meet with
opposition from those of a liberal persuasion. No doubt some
would consider that tougher regulations might impede new business
initiative and might constitute an infringement of the liberties
of the individuals in question. However, it does seem that it is
only too easy for individuals to enter the Colony and establish
a business having provided very little information about themselves
or indeed any proof that the information they do provide is accurate.
It seems to me that it would not be unreasonable to amend the
requirements for providing information when forming a business or
becoming a director in a company, whether newly formed or otherwise.
I do not believe that it would be an undue hardship if the
individuals concerned were required to provide proof of identity
in the form of passport or identity card details and proof of their
address within the jurisdiction. They could also be asked to
provide photographs of themselves. Some might go as far as to say
that fingerprints should also be provided. Although this might
assist police enquiries, I have my doubts as to whether it is really
a necessary requirement. However, it is, already the case in

Hong Kong that before obtaining an identity card, which is mandatory, every applicant must provide fingerprints. So, if it became a requirement that no one could be a company director or a principal in a business without having an identity card, fingerprints would at least be available to the Government and presumably also the police on their request. All information should be open to public inspection as is the scanty information which is presently entered in the Business Names and Companies Registry.

Many countries would be open to this self same criticism, not least of all Panama. In respect of the Panamanian company which owned the good ship "RUST BUCKET" at the time of these frauds the public register showed only the names of the president, secretary and treasurer and gave no addresses. In my submission this is quite inadequate. It has long been regretted, in some quarters, that the identity of shareholders is not revealed in Panamanian public records and those of other countries. Although the anonymity which this provides might be considered to be of considerable benefit to many legitimate businesses it clearly also provides a cloak under cover of which those bent on fraud are unduly protected.

Having more information available in public records would serve a number of useful purposes. It may deter some criminals or at least make life a little more difficult for them. It would enable commercial enterprises to obtain more detailed information with which they could better judge the bona fides of proposed trading partners.

Finally, investigators and the police would have more information available to them and consequently, a better chance of pursuing their enquiries faster and with greater effect with a view to bringing the perpetrators of fraud to justice.

Having said that there is perhaps not enough information available, it is nevertheless the overriding responsibility of those involved in commerce to obtain what information there is and to make proper use of it to protect their own interests.

It is always far too easy to advise on what steps could have been taken when one has the benefit of hindsight. But that doesn't make it any less valuable an exercise. One of the reasons for looking at a case study must be to ask the question, "where did the victims go wrong?".

I will take the victims of these frauds in turn and examine this question. Firstly, we have the vendors of the good ship "RUST BUCKET". Whilst we don't know all the circumstances surrounding the purchase it would appear that they were offered an exceptionally good price. It exceeded the scrap value of the vessel by 50%. Very often marine fraud involves the situation where the victim is offered a special price. For example, a charterer may offer to carry at less than the going freight rates or a supplier may be offering bargain prices. This should put the cautious commercial man on guard, but all too often the effect is exactly the opposite and the inducement works. Regrettably the Taiwanese vendors appeared

to have thrown caution to the wind in the belief that they had
obtained a bargain price. They really should have checked the
credit worthiness of their buyers. If the result would not have
been satisfactory, as seems likely, a request for a guarantee
would surely have been in order. Furthermore, knowing the
appalling condition of the vessel they should not have accepted
her as security for the balance of the purchase price without
at least ensuring that the vessel's hull was insured and that they
would participate in the proceeds of insurance whether by way of
assignment or otherwise, in the event of the vessel being lost.

The Hong Kong bank did not have the benefit of knowing the condition
of the vessel. It appears that they did not arrange an independent
survey and valuation. Had they done so, I doubt whether they would
have loaned US$1 million, which was over six times the vessel's
estimated scrap value. There can be little doubt that the expense
of a survey carried out by a reputable surveyors of their own
choosing would have been money very well spent indeed.

The Iranian consignees of the iron angle bar were not really victims
of fraud. They simply had their cargo stolen by disreputable shipowners. Nevertheless they too could have taken steps to protect
themselves even though they were C & F purchasers and had no
responsibility for arranging the carriage of the cargo. It is not
uncommon for cargo underwriters to specify that the carrying vessel
is warranted not older than a particular age. In my experience

this is never anything like 25 years. This requirement is often passed on to sellers in the purchase contract and could, of course, be incorporated in any event. I would be inclined to recommend purchasers to specify that their goods should not be carried in any vessel built over 15 years before the date of shipment. This is far from a guarantee that the vessel will be sound but at least she may not be knocking on the scrapyard door. Had this been done in this instance, the Korean consignors would not have been entitled to fix the good ship "RUST BUCKET".

In general, consignees and cargo insurers should pay great attention to the vessel upon which it is proposed to ship goods. I am pleased to have observed from instructions my firm has received to investigate proposed carrying vessels and their ownership and management that cargo underwriters are paying much more attention to this aspect of the risk.

In the present case the good ship "RUST BUCKET" was not even to be found in Lloyd's register and this should have alerted anyone dealing with her that something might be amiss or at least to the necessity for further enquiry. When enquiries were commenced by underwriters after the frauds had taken place it took very little time to discover that the vessel apparently had neither hull nor P & I insurers.

I come now to the Singaporean importers, who were probably the best placed to make proper enquiries of their suppliers. I would like

to interpose here some general comments. Sometimes it is
considered by importers that provided that they have obtained
insurance cover they need not concern themselves over much with
ensuring that the cargo arrives at destination. They believe
that if the cargo does not arrive their underwriters will step
in and cover the loss. Unfortunately for them, this is not
the case. All too often marine fraud involves goods which are
purportedly shipped but which never existed. In these circumstances, the risk never attaches and the underwriters are not
liable under the policy. The loss therefore falls on the insured.

It should also be appreciated that buyers cannot rely on their
bankers to protect them by scrutinising documents presented to
them or by enquiring into the question of whether they are genuine.
The banks dealings with the documents are very commonly governed
by the Uniform Customs and Practice of Documentary Credits devised
by the International Chamber of Commerce. These regulations make
it abundantly clear that the banks accept no responsibility for
the authenticity of documents. They are only obliged to check
documents to ensure that they comply with the requirements specified
in Letters of Credit and that they appear on their face to be in order.
They do not have to verify signatures or check whether the vessel
was ever at the load port specified in the Bills of Lading or make
any other enquiry whatsoever.

Given that buyers who finance their purchases by way of Letters of
Credit can expect no acceptance of responsibility or liability from

their bankers and insurers where goods are found never to have existed, the burden of making proper enquiries about their suppliers and the circumstances of the shipment rests firmly and squarely on their shoulders.

In this case study the consignees were dealing with a new supplier and this alone should have indicated that caution was required. Enquiries at the Business Registry and the business premises of Trans Global Trading Corporation would have revealed that despite the grandiose name and impressive note paper of their new found trading partner the buyers were in fact dealing with a newly formed sole proprietorship with very small offices. Further enquiries with credit reference agencies or enquiry agents would have soon indicated that Trans Global Trading Corporation had no track record and were not of any standing.

At this point, many importers might have been inclined to consider other suppliers. But once again we find that the inducement aspect is present. Enquiries revealed that as far as the high density polythene consignments were concerned there was a shortage at the time in question. Other suppliers were not available. Once again, the prospects of making good profits on these consignments may have beguiled the importers into ignoring the inherent risks. After all, they could be heard to say to themselves, many import/ export businesses are very small and many of them have proved to be sound trading partners in the past, so why shouldn't Trans Global Trading Corporation prove to be equally reliable.

However, there were a number of precautions the importers could have taken. The most effective would have been to require that a preshipment survey report and loading certificate be presented as one of the documents required to obtain payment under the Letter of Credit. Ideally, the importers should have appointed the surveyors themselves and asked for a telexed report to go directly to them. This would avoid the risk that Trans Global Corporation could circumvent the requirement by preparing their own forged reports and loading certificates. Generally, it is wise to require documentation from a number of different sources for presentation under Letters of Credit as this makes it difficult for conspirators to obtain the necessary blank forms or to prepare forgeries.

Again it would have been prudent for the Singaporean importers to make enquiries about the identity of the carrying vessel. Had they done so, they would soon have found that she was not listed in Lloyd's register and upon further enquiry they may well have learned of her age and general condition. Having done so, they might have insisted that the cargo be shipped with a reputable shipping line which would have made it rather more difficult for Slick Operators Ltd to produce the necessary Bills of Lading.

Perhaps I can best summarise the morals of this case study as follows :-

1. Commercial men should be cautious when dealing with anyone

A CASE STUDY FROM HONGKONG

offering a special price or someone who purports to be in a position to provide a commodity when others cannot.

2.   It is worth taking the trouble to investigate new trading partners. The modest expense involved may save literally millions of dollars.

3.   It is well worth taking a close interest in the proposed carrying vessel. Often it is found that the vessel does not exist or is nowhere near the port at which she is supposed to be loading.

4.   It is possible to make life more difficult for the would be fraudulent sellers by specifying documents for presentation under Letters of Credit which cannot easily be produced by shippers in collusion with dishonest shipowners.

In short, the guiding principle is still the common law rule, caveat emptor, or, let the buyer beware.

INSURED PERILS, PROXIMATE CAUSE AND THE MARINE INSURANCE ACT

Speaker: Anthony Colman
Queen's Counsel
London

<u>INSURED PERILS, PROXIMATE CAUSE</u>
<u>AND THE MARINE INSURANCE ACT</u>

ANTHONY COLMAN Q.C.

Introduction

The concept of promximate cause sometimes gives rise to
difficult problems in Marine Insurance. Let me start by asking
why it matters what the proximate cause of the loss was. It is
for this reason; that the insurer by his policy agrees to pay
the assured upon the happening of a certain event. But the
event really has two component parts. First the subject-matter
of the insurances, i.e. the vessel, the goods or the freight,
must have been lost or damaged. Secondly, the loss or damage
must have been caused by a peril insured against. That is to say
by one of the fortuitous events expressed in the policy or its
various extensions. It is not every causal relationship which will
be sufficient connection between the insured peril and the loss
and damage.

For example, in one old case decided in 1825, <u>Mordy v. Jones</u>
4 B & C 394, the question arose whether the underwriter who had
insured the freight was liable for loss of part of the freight in
these circumstances. The vessel ISABELLA set out on a voyage from
Kingston, Jamaica to Liverpool with a mixed cargo including cotton,
coffee, sugar and hides. Shortly after commencement of the voyage
she sprang a leak and had to put back to Kingston where the whole
cargo had to be discharged to enable her to carry out repairs.
When they got the cargo off they found that it had got so wet
with seawater that unless it were washed with fresh water and
then dried in the sun before re-loading there would be a danger

of ignition during the course of the voyage. But it would have taken 6 weeks to complete this operation and this could have involved expenses equal to that part of the freight attributable to those goods. The master thereupon sold the goods at Kingston and an arbitrator found that this was a prudent course. The master could not find substitute cargo within a reasonable time and he therefore sailed to Liverpool where he paid over to the receivers the process of Sale of the goods but did not retain from the proceeds any amount in respect of freight. It was argued for the underwriters that the loss of the freight was caused not by any insured peril, in particular perils of the seas, but by the master's decision not to delay the vessel until the cargo was in a fit state to be shipped: it was not the case that an insured peril had prevented the cargo being carried and so prevented the vessel from earning the freight, but merely that the freight had become more expensive to earn and therefore an inconvenience to the shipowners.

The Court of King's Bench agreed with the underwriters. Chief Justice Abbott, that outstanding expert on shipping law, said that merely because the master had taken a prudent decision and the owner thereby lost part of the freight it did not follow that the underwriters were liable.

In that case, but for the perils of the sea causing damage to the cargo, the master would not have been called upon to take the decision which he did but that was not to say that perils of the sea had been the proximate cause of the loss, although it did have some causal connection with the loss of freight.

3

I use the phrase "proximate cause of the loss" because that is how the Marine Insurance Act expresses the principle in section 55(1). I quote

> "Subject to the provisions of this Act, and unless the policy otherwise provides, the insurer is liable for any loss proximately caused by a peril insured against, but subject as aforesaid, is not liable for any loss which is not proximately caused by a peril insured against."

I should now like to discuss with you how the courts have applied this idea of proximate causation in practice.

Loss Proximately caused by Delay

Section 55(2)(b) of the Marine Insurance Act 1906 states I quote:

> "In particular -
>
> (b) Unless the policy otherwise provides, the insurer of ship or goods is not liable for any loss proximately caused by delay, although the delay be caused by a peril insured against."

Ang clause 5 of the Institute Cargo Clauses (All Risks) states: I quote:

> "This insurance is against all risks of loss of or damage to the subject-matter insured but shall in no case be deemed to extend to cover loss damage or expense proximately caused by delay or inherent vice or nature of the subject-matter insured. Claims recoverable hereunder shall be payable irrespective of percentage."

4

That it is not always easy to draw the line between loss
being proximately caused by the insured peril as distinct from
delay brought about by the insured peril is illustrated by some
of the cases.

An easy case is Taylor v. Dunbar (1889) L.R. 4 C.P. 206 in
which the Plaintiff was a meat wholesaler in London who insured
pig and beef carcases on voyages from Hamburg to London in two
vessels. The vessels were subjected to very strong seas and were
obliged to put into Cuxhaven to shelter. They shipped a lot of
water but none of it got on to the cargo. The vessels were
delayed for several days and the meat was found to be putrid.
It was held that although the delay was due to perils of the seas,
the loss was not proximately caused by those perils but by the
delay and that was not an insured peril under the standard
Lloyd's Policy.

A somewhat less obvious case was Pink v. Flemming (1890)
25 Q.B.D. 396. In that case the owner of a cargo of oranges and
lemons claimed on the cargo underwriters under what was then the
F.P.A. Clause which provided

"Warranted free from particular average, unless ship be
stranded, sunk, or burnt, or unless damage be consequent
on collision with any other ship."

Well, a collision did occur, the carrying vessel was damaged and
had to put into port for repairs. In order to carry out repairs
they had to discharge the oranges and lemons into lighters where
they were kept until they could be reloaded after completion of
repairs. The cargo owners claimed against the underwriters
in respect of damage to the cargo. The Court of Appeal held that

the claim failed. Lord Esher M.R. said this:

"In the case of an action for damages on an ordinary contract the defendant may be liable for damage, of which the breach is an efficient cause or causa causans; but in cases of the real insurance only the causa proxima can be regarded. This question can only arise where there is a succession of causes, which must have existed in order to produce the result. Where that is the case, according to the law of marine insurance, the last cause only must be looked to and the others rejected, although the result would not have been produced without them. Here there was such a succession of causes. First there was the collision. Without that no doubt the loss would not have happened. Would such loss have resulted from the collision alone? Is it the natural result of the collision that the ship should be taken to a port for repairs, and that the cargo should be removed for the purposes of the repairs, and that, the cargo being of a kind that must be injured by handling, it should be injured in such removal? A collision might happen without any of these consequences. If it had not been for the repairs, and for the removal of the cargo for the purposes of such repairs, and for the consequent delay and handling of the fruit, the loss would not have happened. The collision may be said to have been a cause, and an effective cause, of the ship's putting into a port and of repairs being necessary. For the purpose of such repairs it was necessary to remove the fruit, and such removal necessarily caused damage to it. The agent, however, which proximately caused

the damage to the fruit was the handling, though no doubt
the cause of the handling was the repairs, and the cause of
the repairs was the collision. According to the English law
of marine insurance only the last cause can be regarded.
There is nothing in the policy to say that the underwriters
will be liable for loss occasioned by that. To connect the
loss with any peril mentioned in the policy, the Plaintiffs
must go back two steps, and that according to English law
they are not entitled to do."

Finally, in cases where the subject matter of the insurance
is not goods or hull but charter freight situations may arise
where the insured peril causes the frustration of the charterparty
because the delay which will elapse before the vessel can be
repaired will be so great that the contract contained in the
charterparty is no longer performable by either party. In that
case it has been held that the loss of the freight which would
otherwise have been earned under that contract has been proximately
caused by the insured peril and not by delay consequent on the
insured peril: see another decision of the Court of Appeal of
which Lord Esher was also a member in Re. Jamieson and the Newcastle
Steamship Freight Insurance Association (1895) 2 Q.B. 90. In these
cases on freight insurance, particularly charter hire insurance,
the courts do tend to play down or exclude delay consequent on
the peril insured against and are much more willing to draw a
direct causal link between the peril and the loss of freight or
hire under the voyage or time charter.

7

Loss Proximately caused by Inherent Vice

Section 55(2) (c) excludes liability on the part of the insurer for amongst other things "inherent vice or nature of the subject-matter insured" - "unless the policy otherwise provides". The sort of thing which is thus excluded is fermentation, bacterial decay, spontaneous combustion and so on. Perishable cargoes are, of coourse, particularly vulnerable by their very nature. It is sometimes very difficult to draw the line between the natural decay of the cargo in the surrounding circumstances of the voyage and the decay of the cargo due to some outside event constituting an insured peril. Let us take a few examples and you will see what I mean.

Take a case such as Wilson Holgate v. Lancashire and Cheshire Insurance Corporation (1922) 13 Ll. L. Rep. 486. Barrels of palm oil were shipped from Singapore to Liverpool. The policy insured against "risks of leakage and breakage from any cause whatsoever irrespective of percentage". Some of the barrels were found at Liverpool to be badly damaged and there had been some leakage from them. Were the insurers liable or were they entitled to deny liability because the barrels were not strong enough to withstand the voyage? Bailhache J, having heard the evidence, held that if the barrels had been properly stowed they would have arrived unharmed. He therefore concluded that the policy protected the assured against the loss by leakage.

The court is really doing this exercise in such cases. It is testing whether there has been some extraneous fortuitous event by ascertaining whether the goods in question had normal characteristics and in particular normal packing for a normal

voyage and whether the method of stowage was normal. If there
was nothing abnormal about the packing on the goods themselves
it might be inferred from the fact of leakage and the actual method
of stowage that the latter was defective. If that was so, it
would be sufficiently an outside event to make the policy pay:
it was not a case of loss proximately caused by the inherent vice
or nature of the goods but by the inadequate method of stowage.

This exercise may prove in practice to be rather difficult.
It may involve a great deal of evidence and in particular
detailed expert evidence from bacteriologists, other scientists and
surveyors. A good illustration of this is the case of Bowring v.
Amsterdam London Insurance Co (1930) 36 Ll. L. Rep. 309. That
was a case of a claim under policies insuring groundnuts on a
voyage from Tsingtao in China to Europe. When the groundnuts
arrived at the discharging ports it was found that they were
damaged because they had overheated in the course of the voyage.
But why? Was this due, as the cargo owners suggested, to sweat
damage due to moisture present in the vessel's cargo spaces or
was it due to the fact that the cargo had an excessively high
moisture content on loading? The policies provided by a special
clause that the insurers were "to pay average and/or damage from
sweating and/or heating when resulting from external cause if
amounting to three per cent in each bag or on the whole". The
court had to decide therefore whether the condition of the
groundnuts did result from an external cause or because to
quote some words of that great commercial law judge, Lord Sumner,
it was "the natural behaviour of that subject matter, being what it
is, in the circumstances under which it is carried". The court
considered a mass of evidence including the exact way in which

the pre-loading survey had been carried out (the Surveyor having certified that the goods were then in good condition and dry), the nature of the cargo surrounding the groundnuts in the stow, the extent to which the holds were ventilated during the voyage, whether there had been any special incidents on the voyage which might have increased the moisture content of the cargo, the methods of harvesting groundnuts in China and of preparing them for shipment, the climatic conditions in the growing areas of China during production of that year's crop, the average moisture content of groundnut cargoes from Tsingtao over eight years and evidence as to the incidence of heating in previous shipments of groundnuts, the bacteriological explanation for fermentation of the cargo and evidence as to the type and spread of damage found by the surveyors at the ports of discharge. Wright J. gave a very long judgment in which he carefully considered all this evidence and came to the conclusion that the damage was due to the unduly high moisture content of the groundnuts at the time of shipment. The claim on the policies therefore failed. I most strongly commend this judgment to anyone, be he assured or insurer, who is concerned with a claim under marine policies in respect of cargo deterioration in defence to which inherent vice has been alleged. If these claims get into the courts they involve a great deal of careful preparation by both sides and depend heavily on expert evidence.

Sometimes it is not the inherent defects of the goods thenselves which may have been the proximate cause of the loss but of the way in which they are packed. The insurers are entitled to say that they are not liable if the shipper had not put the cargo into packing of a kind capable of withstanding the normal incidents of the voyage.

INSURED PERILS, PROXIMATE CAUSE AND THE MARINE INSURANCE ACT

10

A good illustration of this was the case of <u>Berk v. Style</u> (1955) 2 Lloyd's Rep. 382. In that case Kieselguhr was insured under an all risks policy from North Africa to London. This was a bagged cargo and when it got to London it had to be discharged into lighters to be landed. In the course of discharge in slings many of the bags burst and much of the cargo had to be re-bagged before it could be taken out of the lighters. The problem was that the paper bags opened at the seams and the insurers argued that they were not strong enough to withstand ordinary handling on the voyage. Sellers J. found that the bags had not been properly made. The proximate cause of the loss was therefore the defect in packing and not, as the cargo owners contended, the fact that excessive atmospheric moisture in the holds had dissolved the gum which secured the seams of the bags. The proximate cause of the loss was therefore not a peril insured against.

With reference to the limits of protection against fraud which a goods owner purchases when he takes out All Risks Cover, it is as well to remember that the requirement that an extraneous event affecting the goods should be the proximate cause of the loss does somewhat cut down the effect of what is often regarded as a hold-all insurance cover. The first case is not a marine insurance case. In <u>Webster v. General Accident</u> (1953) 1 Q.B. 520 the assured under a motor policy was induced to allow a rogue to drive the car away in reliance on the fraudulent representation made by the rogue that he had a buyer for the car and could sell it for the owner. The rogue then sold it by public auction in his own name and spent the proceeds of sale. There was no hope of recovering the car and the court held that there had been a loss under the policy. But in <u>Eisinger v. General Accident (1955)</u>

11

2 Lloyd's Rep. 95 the facts were slightly difference. The rogue had obtained possession of somebody else's cheque book. He called on the insured who was trying to sell his car and the rogue agreed to buy the car. He gave the insured a cheque out of the book and that, of course, was worthless. The insured then allowed the rogue to take the car away without waiting for the cheque to be cleared. Neither the rogue nor the car were seen again and the insured therefore claimed on his insurers. But he failed to recover. Lord Goddard said that there had simply been no insured loss. What had been lost was not the car at all because unlike the Webster case the insured had intended to transfer title to the rogue. What the assured had lost were the proceeds of sale when the cheque had been dishonoured.

The Webster Case is relevant to cases where the assured is induced to deliver up the cargo to fraudulent transport operators or freight forwarders. In that event they are not intending to pass title to the carrier by their act of delivery but are passing only possession for the purposes of carriage on the voyage necessary to perform the contract under which the goods have been sold. Consequently it does not appear to be likely that under-writers of all risks cover will be able to rely on the argument which succeeded in Eisinger v. General Accident and to contend successfully that what the assured lost was not the goods themselves but merely the price of the goods.

Let me conclude by saying that the principle of the proximate cause is far less important in practice today than earlier in the century when the courts were applying a fairly strict causation analysis particularly to claims under hull

policies arising out of the two World Wars. The result of
these decisions was that the F.C. & S. clause was amended so
as to extend somewhat the cover provided by the Lloyd's
standard hull policy and to make it clear that the proximate
cause of losses by collision stranding and other ordinary
marine perils was not to be treated as a war risk unless it was
caused directly by a hostile act by or against a belligerent power.
Since the F.C. & S. clause is also incorporated into the
Institute Cargo Clauses (F.P.A.), (W.A.) and (All Risks)
it is not likely that many disputes on proximate cause will in
future centre round the F.C. & S. clause. The topic of proximate
cause in the context of war risks is in itself a massive
subject but it is one which seems to me now to be of rather less
general interest at a Seminar of this kind than it would have
been 50 years ago.

The **principle of proximate** causation may strike the
layman as pretty sharp weapon for getting insurers off the hook
but I hope you will agree, having heard this paper, that it has a
reasonably logical foundation which does not work unfairly in
practice provided that it is properly applied.

SHIP-OWNERS DEFENCES TO CARGO CLAIMS

Speaker: Jeremy Russell
Barrister-at-Law
London

SHIPOWNERS' DEFENCES TO CARGO CLAIMS

The title of this talk is "Shipowners' defences to cargo claims". To most people involved with the carriage of goods by sea this would no doubt conjure up images of claims by the owners of cargo carried upon a particular ship against the owners of that ship. Such a claim would be a claim for breach of contract - that is, for breach of the terms of a bill of lading or charterparty. Of course, that is how the majority of cargo claims arise. However, it is worth remembering that a shipowner may face claims for damage to cargo carried not on his own ship, but on someone else's ship or even in respect of cargo ashore. This could happen if, for example, his ship collided with another ship laden with cargo, or collided with a wharf or jetty on which cargo had been stored. In this type of situation the claim against the shipowner will <u>not</u> be for breach of contract - because he will not have a contract with the owners of the cargo carried on the other ship or stored on the wharf - but for the tort of negligence. As we shall see, the distinction may be of importance to the shipowner for a number of reasons.

Before dealing with some of the
specific defences which a shipowner may raise
to cargo claims, I will consider a number of
other matters with which he may be concerned
when such a claim has been made against him.

By whom has the claim been made?

In the case of a claim arising under
a contract the claim which the shipowner
receives may well come from someone with
whom he has, so far as he is aware, never
contracted. However this does not necessarily
mean that the claimant has no right to proceed
against him. How may this come about?

It is a well-established principle
of the law of contract that a person who
has suffered loss or damage as the result
of a breach of contract cannot take legal
action in respect of that breach unless he
was a party to that particular contract.
If applied to the carriage of goods by sea,
this rule could cause great hardship to
cargo-owners. For example, take the situation
where a timber merchant in Singapore sells
some timber to a purchaser in the Middle
East upon C.I.F. terms. As part of the
contract of sale it is his duty as the seller
to arrange shipment of the timber. Accordingly
he will make a contract of carriage with a

shipowner. Let us assume that that contract
is upon the terms of a bill of lading and that
the bill of lading names the Singapore merchant
as shipper and the buyer in the Middle East as
consignee. Whilst the goods are en route to
the Middle East, the buyer takes up and pays
for the documents, pursuant to the contract
of sale. By so doing the buyer becomes the
owner of the goods. On arrival, the timber
is found to have been damaged consequent upon
some breach of the contract of carriage by
the shipowner.

If the general principle which I have
just outlined were to be applied, the result
would be as follows:

-       the buyer, who has paid for sound goods,
        has received damaged goods. However he
        cannot claim against the seller because
        the damage was not caused by any breach
        of the contract of sale.

-       the buyer cannot claim against the
        shipowner because he was not a party
        to the contract of carriage.

-       the seller can claim against the
        shipowner but, as he has been paid
        in full by the buyer, he has suffered
        no loss as a result of the shipowner's
        breach of contract and will be entitled
        only to nominal damages (which for

historical reasons amount to forty

shillings - about nine Singapore dollars).

The result would be the same in the situation
where the consignee had in turn sold the timber
on to some third party and had endorsed and
transferred the bill of lading to that third
party.

From the cargo-owner's point of view
this is clearly unjust. Accordingly the law
relating to bills of lading was changed by the
Bills of Lading Act 1855, which provides by
section 1 that where property in the goods
(in other words ownership of the goods) named
in the bill of lading has passed to the consignee
or indorsee of the bill of lading, then the
shipper's rights and obligations under the
contract of carriage also pass to the consignee
or indorsee. In other words, the consignee or
indorsee is treated as if he were a party
to the contract of carriage - with the result
that he can sue the shipowner for breach of it.
In this way the shipowner may become liable
to some person (for example an indorsee) of
whom he has not previously heard and with whom
he has had no dealings.

Similarly, it has been held that where
a bill of lading has been pledged (for example
to a bank as security for a loan) and the pledgee

(i.e. the bank) presents the bill of lading
to the shipowner and thereby obtains delivery
of the goods, there arises a contract between
the pledgee and the shipowner upon the terms of
the bill of lading. Consequently if the value
of the goods has fallen as the result of some
fault on the part of the shipowner the pledgee
may sue the shipowner for damages.

Thus the moral is: before paying out
on any claim made against him, the shipowner
must satisfy himself that the person who has
made the claim is in fact entitled to do so.
It would be dangerous for him to say "Well I
                ed
contract/with the shipper and only he is entitled
to claim against me" because the contractual
right to claim may have passed from the shipper
to some other party. In that case, payment
to the shipper would not discharge the shipowner's
liability for his breach of contract, with the
result that he might find himself having to
pay twice.

A further point to remember is that
even though the claim is brought by someone
who is ostensibly entitled to do so, in
reality the claimant may well be an underwriter
or insurance company. This situation arises
by virtue of what is known as "subrogation".

A contract of marine insurance is a

contract of indemnity. In other words an assured is not entitled to make a profit out of his insurance - any means by which the loss which he has suffered may be reduced or extinguished must be brought into account. The doctrine of subrogation was developed solely for this purpose, by placing the insurers in the position of the assured. Thus as between the assured and themselves the insurers are entitled "to the advantage of every right of the assured, whether such right consists in contract, fulfilled or unfulfilled, or in a remedy for tort capable of being insisted on or already insisted on, or in any other right, by way of condition or otherwise, legal or equitable, which can be or has been exercised or has accrued, and whether such right could or could not be enforced by them in the name of the assured, by the exercise or acquiring of which right or condition the loss against which the assured is insured can be or has been diminished": per Brett L.J. in Castellain v Preston (1883) 11 Q.B.D. 380 at 388.

The insurer's right of subrogation does not arise until he has made payment under the policy, and even then it must be enforced in the name of the assured. (If the insurer wishes to bring the action in his

own name, he must take an assignment of the
assured's rights against the wrongdoer.)
Thus the insurer is not entitled to make any
claim that the assured himself could not have
made. However, although in reality the insurer
is in control of the legal proceedings, the
law largely ignores the fact that the insurer
is the real plaintiff. For example, the
insurer is not bound to give discovery of
material documents in his own possession,
custody or power but only those documents
in the possession, custody or power of the
assured. Similarly, if the insurer should
lose the action the order for costs is made
against the assured in whose name the action
was brought and not against the insurer. It
is for this reason that the insurer, before
commencing proceedings in the assured's name
will in practice have agreed to indemnify him
in respect of any costs which may be incurred.

Because the rights which pass to the
insurer by way of subrogation are the rights
of the assured the law imposes on the assured
an obligation not to prejudice the position
of the insurers. Thus for example, the
assured may not grant a release to or make
a settlement with the wrongdoer without the
insurer's consent. If, in breach of this
obligation, the assured does grant a release
without his insurer's consent, then either

the insurer is released from liability if he
has not yet paid under the policy, or if he
has already paid, then the assured is liable
either to hand back the insurance payments
or to compensate him in damages.

What is the position of a shipowner
who has been sued, in effect, by the insurer
of the cargo? Well the law will not allow
him to say "the cargo-owner has suffered no
loss, because he has been paid by his insurers,
and so he cannot recover from me", because
that would be to allow the shipowner the
benefit of the cargo-owner's insurance without
having had to pay the premium. Nor can he
resist liability on the ground that the
insurers have paid the assured for a loss in
respect of which they were not liable, provided
that they have acted in good faith. The
reason for this may be found in the speech of
Lord Hobhouse in King v. Victoria Insurance Co.
[1896] A.C. 250 at 254-255:

> "To their Lordships it seems a very
> startling proposition to say that
> when insurers and insured have settled
> the claim of loss between themselves,
> a third party who caused the loss may
> insist on ripping up the settlement,
> and on putting in a plea for the
> insurers which they did not think it
> right to put for themselves; .....

it is claimed as a matter of positive
law that, in order to sue for damage
done to insured goods, insurers must
show that if they had disputed their
liability the claim of the insured
must have been made good against them.
If that be good law, the consequence
would be that insurers could never
admit a claim on which dispute might be
raised except at the risk of finding
themselves involved in the very dispute
they have tried to avoid, by persons
who have no interest in that dispute,
but who are sued as being the authors
of the loss."

But if the policy is void or illegal - for
example if it is a p.p.i. policy - the insurer
is not entitled to be subrogated to any rights
arising in respect of it, even though he has
made a payment under it.

Further even though, as I have said,
the law largely ignores the fact that the
insurer is the real plaintiff, it does not
do so entirely, for the shipowner is entitled
to raise against the insurers a defence which
is available only against them, not against
the nominal plaintiffs. For example, he may
rely upon a term in the policy by which the
insurers have relinquished their rights against

him. Thus in Thomas & Co. v. Brown (1899)
4 Com. Cas. 186, the nominal plaintiffs had
agreed with the defendant lighterman that he
would lighter their goods, which had been
insured by a policy expressed to be "without
recourse to lightermen". The lighter sank
and the insurers, having paid the plaintiffs,
brought an action in their name against the
the defendant. It was held that the defendant
was entitled to rely upon the fact that by the
terms of their policy the underwriters had
relinquished their right to proceed against
lightermen. This defence would not have been
available to him had the action in reality
been brought by the owners of the goods.

Form of action

    Leaving aside the question of arbitration,
the usual form of legal action in all civil
proceedings is an action in personam - that
is, an action brought against the defendant
personally. In this type of action, the writ
must actually be served on the defendant.
Where the defendant shipowner is in fact
a corporation, service is effected (in
Singapore at least) by serving the document
on a director or other officer of the company.

10.

As personal service is required it follows that as a general rule the plaintiff must be within the territorial jurisdiction of the port before proceedings against him can be commenced. However, there are exceptions to this rule and in certain circumstances the Court will give a plaintiff leave to serve proceedings on a defendant who is <u>outside</u> the jurisdiction. Thus with regard to claims arising out of a breach of contract, the rules of the Supreme Court of Singapore will permit service out of the jurisdiction if

(a)   the contract was made within the jurisdiction;   or

(b)   the contract was made by or through an agent trading or residing within the jurisdiction on behalf of a principal trading or residing out of the jurisdiction;   or

(c)   the contract is by its terms or by implication governed by the law of Singapore.

On the other hand, if the claim is one arising out of a collision - for example if the owners of cargo carried on ship A wish to sue the owners of ship B, with which ship A has been in collision - then service out of the jurisdiction will be permitted <u>only</u> if

11.

(a)   the defendant has his habitual residence
      or a place of business in Singapore; or

(b)   the collision occurred within Singaporean
      waters; or

(c)   an action arising out of the same incident
      is proceeding in the   Courts of
      Singapore; or

(d)   the defendant has submitted or agreed
      to submit to the jurisdiction of the
      courts of Singapore.

      As I am sure you can see a plaintiff
cargo-owner could easily find himself in
difficulties. For example, take the case of
my Singaporean timber merchant who ships a
cargo to the Middle East. Suppose that whilst
on the high seas, outside the territorial
waters of any country, the ship upon which his
cargo is being carried is involved in a
collision with a Panamanian registered ship,
whose owner resides in and carries on business
in Greece. Unless the Greek shipowner agrees
to submit to the jurisdiction of the courts
of Singapore, the merchant's only remedy, if
he wishes to proceed in personam, would be
to commence proceedings in Greece. This he
may not wish to do. But does he have any
other option? The answer is "maybe".

      In maritime cases there is another form

of action available, known as an action in rem, from the Latin word "res" meaning "thing" or "object". In this type of action legal proceedings are taken not against a person or a corporation, but against an object - usually a ship - and the writ is served upon the object itself. (Although the owners of the object, where known, must be named in the writ and notice of its issue must be given to them.) An action in rem has two advantages over an action in personam. Firstly, it permits the object against which the writ has been issued to be arrested, thereby ensuring that its owners are unable to remove it from the jurisdiction of the court. Secondly, the plaintiff may ultimately be able to have the res sold in order to satisfy his claim. Thus the plaintiff, by arresting the vessel, obtains a security for his claim which he might well be unable to obtain if his action were in personam.

But how does this help our Singapore timber merchant? Well if the Greek vessel comes into Singapore at any time within two years of the incident, he can issue a writ against the vessel and have it arrested. Alternatively, if the vessel has any sister-ships - that is, ships within the same legal ownership - then if one of those sisterships comes into Singapore, sne may be arrested instead.

(That is one of the reasons why many shipowners arrange their business in such a way that each of their vessels is owned by a separate company - it prevents a sistership arrest.)

Some of you may be wondering why the cargo-owner should go to all this trouble to sue the owner of the _other_ ship, rather than suing the owner of the ship upon which his cargo was being carried, with whom he has a contract. The answer is - because he may not have a cause of action. For example, the crew of the ship upon which his cargo was being carried may not have been to blame for the collision. Even if they were to blame, the terms of the contract of carriage may provide that the shipowner is not to be responsible for the negligent acts of his crew. In such circumstances the cargo-owner's only remedy is to sue the owner of the other ship involved in the collision.

Jurisdiction

Another matter with which a shipowner may well be concerned when a claim is brought against him is whether the tribunal before which the claim has been commenced has jurisdiction to determine the dispute. The shipowner may wish to challenge the jurisdiction

in one of two respects. Firstly, he may wish
to object to the country in which the claim
has been brought - that is, he may wish to
contend that no tribunal within that country
has jurisdiction to determine the dispute.
Alternatively, he may wish to contend that
the particular tribunal before which the action
has been brought has no jurisdiction.

With regard to the first alternative
the position may well differ according to
whether the claim brought against the shipowner
is a claim in tort or a claim for breach of
contract. I will consider first the case of
a claim in tort, and keep to my example of
the Singaporean timber merchant whose cargo
has been damaged consequent upon a collision
between the vessel on which his cargo is being
carried and a Panamanian registered, Greek-
owned vessel. It follows from what I said
a little earlier that the courts of Singapore
would have no jurisdiction to try an action
commenced by the the timber merchant unless
either the Greek owner submitted to the
jurisdiction of the Singapore courts or one
of his vessels was arrested in Singapore.
If, despite the fact that neither of those
conditions had been fulfilled, an action
was commenced in Singapore, the Greek owners
would be entitled to challenge the jurisdiction
of the court and to have the writ set aside.

With regard to contracts, the question
of jurisdiction is commonly determined by the
terms of the contract itself, either expressly
or by implication. An example of an express
choice of jurisdiction is to be found in the
Conline form of bill of lading which provides
that "any dispute arising under this bill of
lading shall be decided in the country where
the carrier has his principal place of business".
An example of an implied choice of jurisdiction
would be a contract which provided that the
laws of a particular country should apply -
the choice of law clause, in the absence of
anything in the contract to the contrary
indicates an agreement to the effect that the
courts of that country shall have jurisdiction.

Suppose that our Singapore timber merchant
contracts, in Singapore, to ship his cargo upon
a Danish vessel on the terms of a Conline
bill of lading. As the contract was made
within Singapore the Singapore court would,
on the face of it, have jurisdiction. But
the parties have agreed that any dispute
arising shall be decided in the place where
the carrier has his principal place of business
- namely Denmark. If the shipowner objected
to having the dispute determined in Singapore,
what would be the position? Does the agreement
to Danish jurisdiction automatically prevent

the Singapore court from hearing the action?
The short answer is no. If the shipowner does
object to Singapore jurisdiction he must apply
for a stay of the action. The court has a
discretion whether or not to grant such a stay,
and in exercising its discretion will be guided
by the following principles:

(i)   where plaintiffs sue in Singapore in
        breach of an agreement to refer disputes
        to a foreign court, and the defendants
        apply for a stay, the Singapore court,
        assuming the claim to be otherwise
        within its jurisdiction, is not bound
        to grant the stay but has a discretion
        whether to do so or not.

(ii)   the discretion should be exercised by
        granting a stay unless strong cause for
        not doing so is shown.

(iii)   the burden of proving such strong cause
        is on the plaintiffs. (In our example,
        the Singapore timber merchant.)

(iv)   in exercising its discretion the court
        should take into account all the
                                   the
        circumstances of A particular case.

(v)   in particular, but without prejudice
        to (iv) the following matters, where
        they arise, may properly be regarded:

        (a)   in what country the evidence on
                the issues of fact is situated,

or readily available, and the effect of that on the relative convenience and expense of trial as between the Singaporean and foreign courts.

(b)   whether the law of the foreign court applies and, if so, whether it differs from the law of Singapore in any material respects.

(c)   with what country either party is connected, and how closely.

(d)   whether the defendants genuinely desire trial in the foreign country, or are only seeking procedural advantages.

(e)   whether the plaintiffs would be prejudiced by having to sue in the foreign court because they would:

(1) be deprived of security for their claim;

(2) be unable to enforce any judgment obtained;

(3) be faced with a time-bar not applicable in Singapore; or

(4) for political, racial, religious or other reasons be unlikely to get a fair trial.

See The Eleftheria [1970] P. 94 at pages 99 - 100 per Brandon J.

18.

Turning to the second type of situation
in which the shipowner may wish to object to
the jurisdiction - namely, where he wishes
to object not to the country in which, but to
the tribunal before which the claim has been
brought. Generally, this problem will occur
only in relation to claims arising out of a
breach of contract. For example the parties
to a voyage charter may have agreed that any
dispute arising under the charterparty will
be submitted to arbitration. Let us assume
that cargo belonging to the voyage charterer
is damaged, and that he commences court
proceedings against the shipowner despite the
arbitration clause. What may the shipowner
do? Well one thing he could do is agree that,
despite the arbitration clause, the claim
should proceed by way of an action in court.
But if he does not want the matter determined
by the court, what is the position? The
answer in Singapore is: provided that he has
not taken any step in the court proceedings
and that he is ready and willing to do all
things necessary to the proper conduct of
the arbitration, the shipowner may apply to
the court for a stay of those proceedings.
However, the court has a discretion whether
or not it will grant such a stay. The position
used to be the same in England. However, by
virtue of Section 1 of the Arbitration Act 1975

where the arbitration is a non-domestic one
- in other words, one of the parties to the
arbitration agreement is a national of or
habitually resident in or a company incorporated
in some state other than the U.K. - the court
must grant a stay, provided that :

(1)   the defendant has not taken any step
       in the proceedings;

(2)   the arbitration is not null and void,
       inoperative or incapable of being
       performed; and

(3)   there is a dispute between the parties
       with regard to the matter agreed to be
       referred.

But why should a shipowner go to the
trouble of seeking to have court proceedings
stayed in favour of arbitration proceedings?
One possible answer lies in the next topic
with which I wish to deal, namely:

Security

As a general rule defendants in court
actions and respondents in arbitration
proceedings do not have to put up security
in respect of the claims made against them.
Nevertheless it may often be prudent for a
shipowner to put up security in respect of
a cargo claim when requested by the cargo

owners to do so. Why? Well the short
answer is the action in rem. If the claim
is one in respect of which such an action
could be commenced, the shipowner is likely
to find that unless he accedes to the cargo-
owner's demand for security, he will soon find
his vessel under arrest. Once that happens
he will be faced with a choice of either leaving
the vessel under arrest until the action has
been tried (which could well take several years)
or of putting up security to get his vessel
released. If a vessel is trading profitably
then the threat of arrest is frequently enough
to cause security to be put up.

But how much security does the shipowner
have to put up? What if the cargo-owner is
demanding sums out of all proportion to his
likely claim? The cargo-owner is entitled
to sufficient security to cover the amount of
his claim together with interest and costs,
on the basis of his reasonably arguable best
case. (cf. The Moschanthy [1971] 1 Lloyd's 37.)
If he demands more than that the shipowner's
remedy lies in an application to the court,
for the court has power to control the amount
of security to be provided in an action in rem.
Thus if the vessel is already under arrest the
shipowner can apply for the vessel's release
againgst the provision of security in an amount

determined by the court. If the vessel is not yet under arrest. it will often be prudent for the shipowner to put up the security demanded, however excessive, and then apply to the court to have the amount of security "moderated".

Nevertheless a shipowner should not be in a hurry to accede to requests for security every time his ship is threatened with arrest. He should first satisfy himself that the cargo-owner is in fact entitled to arrest his ship. For example, suppose that the dispute between the cargo-owner and the shipowner is of a kind which they have agreed should be referred to arbitration. If the cargo-owner commenced court proceedings the shipowner could, as we have seen, apply to the court for a stay. But why should he bother to do that? The answer is - because it is well-settled that proceedings in rem cannot be used merely as a means of compelling a shipowner to put up security in respect of disputes which are to be settled by arbitration. (cf. The Cap Bon [1967] 1 Lloyd's 543: The Maritime Trader [1981] 2 Lloyd's 153.)

However, this does not mean that a cargo-owner who has agreed to submit his dispute to arbitration is always left unsecured, because the last few years have seen the development of something known as the "Mareva

Injunction". Full discussion of this useful
creature would take most of the afternoon and
so I will just give a bare outline of it.
An injunction is an order of the court to do
or, more usually, not to do a particular thing.
A Mareva Injunction is an order of the court
restraining a person from dealing with his
assets in order to prevent their being removed
from the jurisdiction so as to render a final
judgment valueless. In other words, a Mareva
Injunction effectively freezes the assets of
the person against whom it is directed. The
grant of such an injunction is within the
discretion of the court, and before obtaining
such an injunction the plaintiff will have to
establish:

(a)   that he has a substantive claim which
        either

        (i)   it has been agreed will be
                arbitrated within the jurisdiction,
                or

        (ii)   is of a type for which he would be
                granted leave to serve out of the
                jurisdiction.

(b)   that he has a good arguable case with
        regard to his substantive claim.

(c)   that the person against whom he is
        claiming has assets within the jurisdiction
        which that person could easily remove.

(d)   that there is a real risk that those

assets·will be removed from the

jurisdiction before a final judgment

or award is obtained.

Because of the potentially shattering
effect such an order could have upon a person's
business, it is usual to limit the scope of
the injunction to sufficient of his assets to
meet the claim against him, together with
interest and costs. A fairly common form
of order would be as follows:

"It is ordered and directed that the

defendants whether by themselves,

their servants or agents or otherwise

howsoever be restrained, and an

injunction is hereby granted restraining

them from removing from the jurisdiction

or otherwise disposing of and/or dealing

with any of their assets within the

jurisdiction as reduce the total amount

thereof retained within the jurisdiction

below US$500,000 until after payment

by the defendants of the award made in

the intended arbitration or until

further order."

How does all this affect a shipowner?
Well a ship is an asset. Consequently there
is nothing to prevent the court from granting

a Mareva Injunction restraining the shipowner
from removing his vessel from the jurisdiction.
Further, the court may grant such an injunction
in circumstances where the claimant would _not_
be entitled to proceed by way of an action in
rem - for example, where it had been agreed
the dispute should be referred to arbitration.
Thus although a claimant cannot arrest a
vessel in order to obtain security in respect
of arbitration proceedings there is nothing
to prevent him from obtaining a Mareva Injunction
against the vessel for that purpose (cf. The
Rena K [1979] Q.B. 377). The practical result
is that the shipowner will have to
put up security in order to get the injunction
lifted and his vessel released. Another
situation in which a Mareva Injunction may be
used against a shipowner is where his vessel
has been lost and he makes a claim upon his
underwriters - the injunction can be used
to prevent him from removing the proceeds
of the insurance policy from the jurisdiction
until proceedings against him have been
determined.

However there are two important
differences between a Mareva Injunction and
an action in rem. The first is that the
mere service of proceedings in rem upon the
res gives the court jurisdiction. On the

other hand, the court cannot grant a Mareva
Injunction unless it already has jurisdiction.
The second is that the issue of proceedings in
rem puts the plaintiff in the position of a
secured creditor (see The Aro [1980] Ch. 196)
whereas the grant of a Mareva Injunction merely
restricts certain (but not all) dealings with
the assets against which the order has been
made, and most certainly does not put the
plaintiff in the position of a secured creditor.

Time

As a general rule a person who wishes
to bring a claim in either contract or tort
must commence proceedings either in court
or, if applicable, by way of arbitration
within six years from the date on which his
cause of action accrued - that is, the date
on which the breach of contract took place
or the tort was committed. However, in the
case of maritime claims the general rule
frequently does not apply and the time within
which claims must be brought is often much
shorter. Thus where there has been a
collision and the owner of cargo carried on ship
A wishes to sue the owner of ship B, he must
commence his proceedings within two years of
the date of the collision. If the claim is
one for breach of a contract to which the
Hague or the Hague-Visby Rules apply, the

claim must be made within one year. An

extreme example would be a charterparty

containing an unamended Centrocon arbitration

clause, which bars any claim if the claimant's

arbitrator is not appointed within three months

Paragraph. of final discharge.// What happens to the claim

if proceedings are not commenced within the

appropriate time? Can the shipowner sit back

and relax, secure in the knowledge that the

claim has become time-barred? The answer is

"not necessarily". Taking first the claim

of the owner of cargo whose goods have been

damaged consequent upon a collision. If he

fails to commence his proceedings within two

years, nevertheless the court _may_ extend that

time by such period and upon such conditions

as it thinks just and _shall_ do so if satisfied

that during the two-year period there had

been no reasonable opportunity of arresting

the defendant vessel within the jurisidction

of the court or within the territorial waters

of the country in which the claimant resides

or has his principal place of business. On

the other hand, it has been held that Article

III rule 6 of the Hague Rules which provides

(inter alia) that "the carrier and the ship

shall be discharged from all liability .....

unless suit is brought within one year",

does not merely bar the right to claim,

but extinguishes it entirely. (cf. _Aries_

27.

Tanker Corporation v. Total Transport Limited
[1977] 1 W.L.R. 185.)

The position with regard to time limits
laid down in arbitration clauses is different
again. Here, even though the time limited for
commencing arbitration proceedings has expired,
the court has power, if it is of opinion that
in the circumstances of the case undue hardship
would be caused if the claim was not allowed
to proceed, to extend that time for such period
and upon such terms as it thinks just. In
determining whether undue hardship would be
caused, the court will keep in mind the
following:

(1)   the words "undue hardship" should not
      be construed too narrowly.

(2)   undue hardship means excessive hardship
      and, where the hardship is due to the
      fault of the claimant, it means hardship
      the consequences of which are out of
      proportion to such fault.

(3)   in deciding whether to extend time or
      not, the court should look at all the
      relevant circumstances of the particular
      case.

(4)   in particular, the following matters
      should be considered:

      (a)   the length of the delay:

28.

(b)   the amount at stake;

(c)   whether the delay was due to the
       fault of the claimant or to
       circumstances outside his control;

(d)   if it was due to the fault of the
       claimant, the degree of such
       fault;

(e)   whether the claimant was misled
       by the other party;

(f)   whether the other party has been
       prejudiced by the delay and, if
       so, the degree of such prejudice.

(per Brandon J. in The Jocelyne [1977]
2 Lloyd's 121.)

It is not at all uncommon for a
charterparty to include both an arbitration
clause and, by way of the clause paramount,
the Hague Rules. If, as I have said, the
effect of Article III rule 6 is not merely
to bar the claim but extinguish it entirely,
can the court nevertheless, in the exercise
of the power to which I have just referred,
extend the time for the commencement of
arbitration proceedings? The short answer
is yes. Although this answer may seem somewhat
surprising, nevertheless that is the effect
of the statute giving the court power to extend
time in cases of undue hardship: The Virgo
[1978] 2 Lloyd's 167.

Before leaving the question of time, there is one other matter to which I wish to refer, and that is the question of extensions of time. Where the claim has been made against a shipowner it is not uncommon for him to be asked to grant an extension of the time for commencement of proceedings. What should he do in that situation? There are a number of reasons why a shipowner might decide to grant such an extension. For example, if the claimant is one with whom the shipowner does a large amount of business, he may be prepared to grant the claimant an extension of time as a gesture of goodwill. Another example would be where negotiations to settle the dispute are in progress and rather than force the claimant to commence proceedings merely to keep time open, the shipowner grants an extension in the hope that the negotiations will come to a satisfactory conclusion and legal proceedings will thereby be avoided altogether. Thus no definite answer, applicable to all cases, can be given. In the final analysis, the decision to grant or not to grant an extension of time will be based upon commercial rather than legal considerations.

Having satisfied himself that the person claiming against him has the right to claim, that the claim has been brought before

the proper tribunal and within the proper
time, the shipowner can then turn his
attention to the question of what defences
might be open to him.

Tort

Where the claim against the shipowner
arises out of damage to cargo upon another
vessel consequent upon a collision with his
own vessel, the shipowner's options are
limited. If, as will usually be the case,
both vessels are to blame the shipowner will
be unable to resist the cargo-owner's claim.
However, there are several points worth
remembering:

(1)   in English law the cargo carried on
       board a ship is identified with the
       fault of that ship. For example,
       suppose there is a collision between
       ship A fully laden, and ship B, in
       ballast, for which ship A is 75 per
       cent and ship B 25 per cent to blame.
       If the owners of cargo lost or damaged
       as a result of the collision sue the
       owners of ship B, they will be able
       to recover only 25 per cent of their
       loss. (see The Milan (1860) Lush 388
       approved in The Drumlanrig [1911]
       A.C. 16.)

(2)   in the U.S. the position is different

- there, the owner of cargo carried on ship A can recover the whole of his loss from the owner of ship B: see, for example, The Anco Princess [1978] 1 Lloyd's 293.

(3)   if the owner of ship B is sued by the cargo-owner in a jurisdiction (such as the U.S.) in which he is compellable to pay the cargo claim in full, he may be able to reclaim a proportion of that claim from the owner of ship A: The Giacinto Motta [1977] 2 Lloyd's 221.

(4)   the shipowner will be able to limit his liability under the provisions of the Merchant Shipping Acts, provided that the collision was not caused or contributed to by any actual fault or privity on his part.

Contract

Where the claim against the shipowner arises out of an alleged breach of the contract of carriage the defences available to him will depend upon the terms of the contract and the circumstances of the particular case. As both of these are almost infinitely variable - in theory, at least - I will restrict myself to some of the more common contractual defences. Before doing so, however, I have a few words to say about the

onus of proof.

Onus of proof   It is for the cargo owner
to establish that loss of or damage to his
goods has occurred during a period in which
they were within the care or custody of the
shipowner. Once that has been established
it is for the shipowner, if he wishes to
avoid liability, to establish that the loss
or damage was caused by some event for which
he is not legally responsible. For example,
if cargo has been damaged and there is doubt
as to whether that damage was caused by bad
stowage (liability for which, let us assume,
is not excluded by the terms of the contract)
or by perils of the sea, it will be for the
shipowner to establish that the damage was in
fact caused by perils of the sea. If he
fails to do so, he will be liable. Similarly,
where two separate causes have contributed
to the loss or damage and liability for only
one of those causes is excepted by the terms
of the contract, it is for the shipowner to
establish which part of the loss or damage
which was caused by the excepted cause and
which was not. (See, for example, The Europa
[1908] P. 84.)

On the other hand, once the shipowner
establishes that the loss or damage was the
result of some excepted event, the burden

33.

of showing that he is not entitled to the
benefit of that exception, for example on the
ground of negligence, falls upon the cargo-
owner. (See, for example, The Glendarrock
[1894] P. 226.)

     Returning to defences, because they are
so widely employed both in bills of lading
and charterparties I will consider first the
defences available under the Hague Rules.

Hague Rules The carrier's defences are to
be found in Article IV of the Rules. However,
one cannot consider these without first
considering the operation of Article III rule
1, because "Article III rule 1 is an overriding
obligation. If it is not fulfilled and the
non-fulfillment causes the damage the immunities
of Article IV cannot be relied on:" per Lord
Somervell in   Maxine Footwear v. Canadian
Government Merchant Marine [1959] A.C. 589.
(Although strictly true, this statement could
mislead some people into believing that a
breach of Article III rule 1 would leave a
shipowner wholly defenceless. That is not
in fact the position, because even if he is
in breach of that rule, the shipowner can
still rely upon the limitation provisions in
Article IV rule 5 and, in an appropriate case,
upon the provisions of Article IV rule 6.)

Article III rule 1 provides:

"The carrier shall be bound, before and
at the beginning of the voyage, to
exercise due diligence to -

(a) make the ship seaworthy;

(b) properly man, equip and supply
the ship;

(c) make the holds, refrigerating and
cool chambers, and all other
parts of the ship in which goods
are carried, fit and safe for their
reception, carriage and preservation."

I will consider some of the elements of that
rule very briefly:

(1)   <u>Before and at the beginning of the</u>
<u>voyage</u>.
There words cover the period from at
least the beginning of loading until
the vessel starts upon her contractual
voyage - that is, the voyage from the
port of loading to the port of
discharge as described in the particular
bill of lading upon which the shipowner
is being sued: <u>Maxine Footwear case</u>,
supra; <u>The Makedonia</u> [1962] 1 Lloyd's
316. Accordingly, a shipowner who
has exercised due diligence to make
his ship seaworthy in all respects
before she sails on the contractual

voyage will not be liable for defects
rendering the veseel unseaworthy which
arise _after_ the vessel has sailed.
For example, in The Chyebassa [1966]
2 Lloyd's 193, goods shipped from
Calcutta to Rotterdam arrived damaged
by seawater owing to stevedores having
stolen a storm valve coverplate during
the unloading and loading of other cargo
at Port Sudan. Although the vessel
was therefore unseaworthy on leaving
Port Sudan, the plaintiffs' allegation
that the shipowners were in breach of
Article III rule 1 failed on the
shipowners proving that they had exercised
due diligence to make the vessel seaworthy
before and at the commencement of the
contractual voyage from Calcutta.

(2)   Due diligence to make the ship seaworthy.
Due diligence means reasonable diligence
having regard to the circumstances as
known or to be expected, taking into
account the nature of the voyage and
the cargo to be carried. It is not
enough that the shipowner has _personally_
been diligent - the rule requires that
diligence to make the vessel seaworthy
shall _in fact_ have been exercised.
Thus a shipowner will not escape liability
even where, for example, he has exercised

36.

due diligence to appoint a reputable
shiprepairer and the cause of the unseaworthiness
is the fault of that repairer: Riverstone
Meat Co. Pty. Ltd. v. Lancashire Shipping
Co.Ltd. [1961] A.C. 807. In reality,
what this means is that if there is some
physical defect in the vessel rendering
it unseaworthy the shipowner will be
liable unless he can establish that it
was latent, i.e. was one which would not
have been revealed by an inspection of a
character such as a reasonably prudent
shipowner would have made and carried
out with reasonable skill and care.

(3)   Properly man, equip and supply the ship.
The shipowner must satisfy himself that
his crew are reasonably fit to occupy
the posts to which they are appointed.
Thus in The Makedonia, supra, Hewson J.
said in relation to the selection of
offices:

> "In my view, the least that should
> be done is to ensure a careful
> inspection of the seaman's book,
> to study the history of the
> applicant and to question him
> about it and the reason why he
> left his former ships; if, for
> example, he appears to have sailed
> one voyage, one owner, the

certificate ought to be sighted -
the certificate might have been
suspended. Enquiry should be made
of previous owners, and if the
report says 'nothing against him',
to press for fuller information.
I cannot imagine anything more
damning than a report from a previous
owner that he had 'nothing against
him'. If nothing confidential is
forthcoming the man should be interviewed
until the interviewer is reasonably
satisfied about him and, if he is
not satisfied, he should reject him.
Such important appointments to such
responsible positions call for a
proper interviewing and a proper
enquiry."

It has been held that it is not enough merely
to rely upon the fact that the crew member
concerned held an appropriate certificate of
competency; The Farrandoc [1967] 2 Lloyd's
276.

Whether due diligence has been exercised
is a matter of fact in each case. However, no
onus to prove that he exercised due diligence
is cast upon the shipowner until the cargo-
owner has proved to the satisfaction of the
court that (i) the vessel was unseaworthy and
(ii) his goods suffered damage as a result of
that unseaworthiness.

38.

Turning to Article IV, the ship owner's main defences are to be found in the 17 sub paragraphs of Rule 2. I will go through these fairly quickly, just to highlight some of the points which a ship owner needs to keep in mind.

(a)   Act, neglect, or default of the master, mariner, pilot, or the servants of the carrier in the nagivation or in the management of the ship.

There are two questions which have arisen as to the scope of this exception. The first is: over what period does it operate. Does it apply only to acts whilst the vessel is actually in the course of navigating from one port to another? The answer would appear to be that the exception applies to the whole of the contractual voyage - that is, from the commencement of loading to the completion of discharge.

The second area of uncertainty has been as to the precise scope to be given to the words "management of the ship". After all, many acts or omissions by those on board may affect cargo. To give just two examples, failure to operate hold ventilation machinery and the failure to ascertain the condition of the ballast tanks and lines before ballasting down are both failures to operate the ship's machinery correctly, which have resulted in damage to cargo. Nevertheless, whilst the latter has been held to be a fault in the management of the ship, with the result that the ship owner was exempt from liability, the former has been held not to be a fault in the management of the ship. Wherein lies the difference between these two cases? The answer is that a distinction has to be drawn between those acts or omissions which constitute want of care of cargo and those which constitute a want of care of the vessel indirectly affecting cargo.

Thus, to give a few more examples, failure to get rid of water
from a hold after a collision, failure to take hold soundings and a
failure to use locking bars on the hatches at sea in heavy
weather have been held to be " acts, neglects or defaults in the
management of the ship". On the other hand, leaving hatches open
to allow easy access to repair workers, whereby rain entered the
holds and damaged the cargo, and failure properly to secure or
stow cargo have been held not to be "acts, neglects or defaults
in the management of the ship".

(b)   Fire, unless caused by the actual fault or privity
of the carrier.

        This exemption is similar to that provided by
Section 502 of the Merchant Shipping Act 1894. However, there
are important differences. The first is that the Section 502
exemption is limited to British ships, whereas the Hague Rules
exemption is not. Second is that the Hague Rules exemption cannot
be relied upon in circumstances where the fire was caused by
unseaworthiness, whereas the Section 502 exemption can be relied
upon in such circumstances, provided only that there was no
actual fault or privity on the part of the ship owner. Thus where
cargo has been lost or damaged as the result of a fire on board
ship, the prudent ship owner will rely upon both exemptions, if
it is open to him to do so.

(c)   Perils, dangers and accidents of the sea or other
navigable waters.

        There are three main points to note here. The first
is that "perils of the sea" denotes accidents peculiarly incident
to navigating the sea. As Lord Esher said in Pandorf v Hamilton

(1866) 17 QBD 670, perils of the sea "really are the perils to which people who carry on business on that dangerous element are liable because they carry on their business on the sea. They are the perils of the sea, not the perils of journeying". Thus loss of or damage to goods by sea water, storms, collision, stranding, pirates and collision with natural objects such as icebergs or with other vessels would prima facie be losses by perils of the seas.

The second point is that the incident giving rise to the loss or damage must be accidental or fortuitous. The classic statement of the law on this point is that of Lord Herschell in Hamilton and Pandorf (1887) 12 AC 518:

> "It is well settled that it is not every loss
> or damage of which the sea is the immediate cause,
> that is covered by these words. They do not
> protect, for example, against the natural and
> inevitable action of the winds and waves which
> result in what may be described as wear and tear.
> There must be some casualty, something which could
> not be foreseen as one of the necessary incidents
> of the adventure."

To give a recent example from Canada, in Crippen & Associates Ltd v Vancouver Tug Boat Co. [1971] 2 Lloyds 207, a cargo of peat moss was loaded in good order and condition on to the Defendant's barge at Nadu, B.C. . Upon discharge from the barge at Vancouver the cargo was found to have been damaged by sea water. The Defendant relied upon Article IV, Rule 2 (c). The Judge found that "in the present case the evidence was to the effect that the weather was not abnormal for the time of year, that the voyage was

41.

accomplished in the normal time without the necessity of slackening speed or changing course, and that while the cargo was subjected to the usual vibration which could be anticipated in a tow of this nature, it had not shifted or fallen due to not being firmly packed, but that the damage was due to other factors rather than to the action of the wind and waves, which was not abnormal". Accordingly the Defence failed.

The final point is that even though the loss was caused by an incident properly characterised as a peril of the sea and which arose fortuitously, nevertheless the ship owner will not be able to rely upon this exemption if the loss or damage would not have occurred but for the negligence of the ship owner or his employees. Thus although I have said that damage resulting from collision with an iceberg would prima facie be a loss by perils of the sea, nevertheless the ship owner would not be protected if the cause of that collision was the negligence of those navigating his vessel. Similarly if the reason sea water damage occurred was because the vessel was unseaworthy, the ship owner cannot rely upon this exemption.

(d)   Act of God.

The classic definition is that of James, LJ. in Nugent v Smith (1876) 1 CPD 423:

> "The Act of God is a mere short way of
> expressing this proposition: a common carrier
> is not liable for any accident as to which he
> can show that it is due to natural causes,
> directly and exclusively, without human inter-
> vention, and that it could not have been prevented

by any amount of foresight and pains and care
reasonably to be expected from him".

There is clearly an overlap between this exception and the previous
one - an unusually violent storm for example would be both a
peril of the sea and an Act of God. On the other hand, this
exception would also cover such things as damage by lightning or
by frost, which are not perils peculiar to the sea.

(e)   Act of war.

(f)   Act of public enemies.

These require little explanation. "War" has been held
not to have a technical meaning. Thus it would cover not only
situations where war has formally been declared but also civil
war and acts done in the course of hostilities between states
between whom diplomatic relations have not been severed.

(g)   Arrest or restraint of Princes, rulers or people, or
seizure under legal process.

(h)   Quarantine restrictions

"Arrest or restraints of Princes, Rulers and Peoples"
covers forceable interferences with the voyage or adventure by
the Government or ruling power of a country, whether done by it
as an enemy of the state to which the vessel belongs or not. Thus
the exception will cover such things as prohibitions on the
import or export of certain types of goods, embargoes on goods
shipped to or from a particular country or upon particular ships,
quaratine regulations and so on. Further, potential as distinct
from actual interference can constitute a restraint. Thus a ship
owner can rely on this exception even though the vessel is outside

43.

the jurisdiction of the state imposing the restraint, provided
that he is subject to the jurisdiction of that state, either
because he is physically within its territory or because he is
a subject of it: Furness Withy v Rederiaktiegolabet Banco [1917]
2 KB 873.

The second part of the exception - seizure under
legal process - will protect the ship owner where, for example,
the vessel is arrested at the suit of the owners of cargo carried
upon a previous voyage, or by charterers. This was added because
it had long been held that the bare exception "arrest or
restraint of Princes, rulers or people", commonly found in charter
party exclusion clauses, did not apply to arrest or seizures
resulting from ordinary legal process.

(i)   Acts or omission of the shipper or owner of the
goods,his agent or representative.

Loss or damage arising from the act of the shipper
or owner will usually be the result of such things as inadequate
packing or marking of the goods, and these are matters covered
by other exceptions. Thus this paragraph is in effect a sweeping
up provision to give the ship owner protection when the loss or
damage is the result of some act or omission of the shipper or
owner which is not specifically covered elsewhere in the rules.

(j)   Strikes or lock outs or stoppage or restraint of
labour from whatever cause, whether partial or general.

The meaning of this clause is reasonably plain, and
the Courts have, in recent years at least, taken a fairly broad
view as to what constitutes a strike, thus in The New Horizon [1975]

44.

2 Lloyds 314: the vessel arrived at St. Nazaire where it was customary for crane and sucker drivers to work in shifts and thereby provide a 24 hour service, although not required by their contracts of employment to do so. However, at the time of the vessels' arrival the drivers were, as part of a campaign to improve their conditions of employment, working only during the day and refusing all shift work. The Court held that the refusal of the drivers to work shifts was a "strike", even though that refusal was limited to only a portion of the day and even though they were not in breach of their contracts of employment in insisting on day work only. In that case Lord Denning, MR., defined a strike as follows:

> "I think a strike is a concerted stoppage of work by men done with a view to improving their wages or conditions, or giving vent to a grievance or making a protest about something or other, or supporting or sympathising with other workmen in such endeavour. It is distinct from a stoppage which is brought about by an external event such as a bomb scare or by apprehension of danger".

(k)   Riots and civil commotions.

The word "riots" is here used in its strict legal sense. A riot is defined - perhaps somewhat quaintly - as :

> "A tumultuous disturbance of the peace by three or more persons, who assemble together, without lawful authority, with an intent mutually to assist one another, by force if necessary, against

any who shall oppose them in the execution

of a common purpose and who actually execute,

or begin to execute that purpose in a violent

manner displayed not merely by demolishing

property but in such a manner as to alarm at

least one person of reasonable firmness and

courage".

The phrase "civil commotions" is used to indicate the stage between a riot and a civil war. It has been defined to mean an insurrection of the people for general purposes, although not amounting to rebellion; but it is probably not capable of any very precise definition. The element of turbulence or tumult is essential; an organised conspiracy to commit criminal acts where there is no tumult or disturbance until after the act, does not amount to a civil commotion.

(1)   Saving or attempting to save life or property at sea.

(m)   Wastage in bulk or weight or any other loss or damage arising from inherent defects, quality or vice of the goods.

These are largely self explanatory.

(n)   Insufficiency of packing.

What is meant here is that the goods were insufficiently packed to withstand such handling as they were likely to undergo in the normal course of the adventure.

(o)   Insufficiency or inadequacy of marks.

This is a narrow exception and will only protect the
ship owner if he can prove (i) that the goods are unidentifiable
owing to insufficiency of marks and (ii) that he has not lost
any of them, or if he has, that they were lost by some other
excepted peril.

(p)   Latent defects not discoverable by due diligence.

Latent defects means latent defects in the ship, not
in the goods which are the subject of the claim. It may also cover
latent defects in shore appliances such as cranes and perhaps even
in other cargo. A defect is latent if it is one which could not
be discovered by a competent person exercising reasonable skill
and care. As by definition a latent defect is one which could not
have been discovered by the exercise of due diligence the ship
owner will, in appropriate circumstances, be entitled to rely upon
this exception even though he cannot prove that he had exercised
due diligence.

(q)   Any other cause arising without the actual fault
or privity of the carrier, or without the fault or neglect of the
agents or servants of the carrier, but the burden of proof shall
be on the person claiming the benefit of this exception to show
that neither the actual fault or privity of the carrier nor the
fault or neglect of the agents or servants of the carrier contributed to the loss or damage.

This is a sweeping up provision which entitles the
ship owner to protection provided that the loss was not caused by
negligence. That proviso is important, because although the ship

47.

owner does not have to show the precise cause of the loss or damage, his defence will fail if the cause remains wholly unexplained. A classic example is the case of <u>Pendle and Rivet v Ellerman Lines</u> (1927) 33 Com.Cass. 70, where the plaintiffs had shipped a case containing wool and silk goods on the defendants' vessel. On arrival the case was found to contain old newspapers. The Court was satisfied that the loss occurred while the goods were in the defendants' custody. As the defendants were unable to give <u>any</u> explanation as to how the loss occurred they were unable to prove that it had occurred without the negligence of their servants or agents. Consequently, the defence under this paragraph failed.

There are two final points which I would like to make with regard to the defences available under Article IV Rule 2. The first is that the ship owner cannot rely upon these exceptions for loss or damage caused by his negligence or, save as provided by Paragraphs (a) and (b), that of his servants or agents. The second is that the ship owner cannot rely upon these exceptions if there has been a deviation unless that deviation is of such a character as to fall within Article IV Rule 4, which provides:

> "Any deviation in saving or attempting to save
> life or property at sea or any reasonable
> deviation shall not be deemed to be an infringe-
> ment or breach of these Rules or of the contract
> of carriage, and the carrier shall not be liable
> for any loss or damage resulting therefrom".

However, this is largely academic in view of the broad deviation clauses usually to be found in Bills of Lading.

Singapore is a party to the 1968 Protocol amending the Hague Rules. With regard to the defences available to the ship owner under the Hague-Visby Rules, as the amended Rules are known, the main points to note are as follows:

(i)   The defences available under Article IV Rule 2 remain the same but are now available not only to the ship owner but also to his servants or agents (but not to his independent contractors).

(ii)   The ship owner is not entitled to the benefit of the limitation provision in Article IV Rule 5 if it is proved that the loss of or damage to the cargo resulted from his act or omission done with intent to cause damage, or recklessly and with knowledge that the damage would probably result. There is a similar provision removing protection from servants and agents if they have caused the damage intentionally or recklessly. The burden of proving such intention or recklessness will be upon the cargo owner.

(iii) The limit of liability has been changed from £100 to 10,000 gold francs per package or unit and 30 gold francs per kilo of gross weight of the goods lost or damaged, and there is some attempt to clarify the meaning of "package or unit" where goods are

49.

consolidated in containers or upon pallets.

Charter Parties

What I am concerned with here today is ship owners' defences to cargo claims. In the case of time charter parties the time charterer has usually hired the vessel to try and make a profit by shipping goods belonging to others, rather than to ship his own goods. Where the time charterer procures cargo for the vessel the bills of lading are commonly signed for and on behalf of the master, thereby bringing about a contract upon the terms of the bill of lading between the shipper and the ship owner. Thus when a cargo claim is brought against the ship owner it is usually brought by the shipper or consignee named in or an indorsee of the bill of lading, not by the time charterer. Indeed when there is a claim for loss or damage to goods carried upon a time chartered ship, it will normally be the time charterer who is trying to defend a claim for an indemnity brought by the ship owner, rather than the ship owner trying to defend a cargo claim brought by the time charterer. However, this is not to say that a ship owner will never be faced with a claim for loss of or damage to cargo brought by a time charterer. In that even- tuality, what defences are available to him? The answer will depend upon the terms of the particular contract, and I will look very briefly at two common forms of time charter.

New York Produce Exchange Form

Clause 16 provides (inter alia) as follows:

"The Act of God, enemies, fire, restraint of Princes, Rulers and People, and all dangers and accidents of the Seas, Rivers, Machinery, Boilers and Steam Navigation, and errors of navigation

throughout this charter party, always   mutually

excepted".

We have considered many of these exceptions already when looking

at the defences provided by Article IV of the Hague Rules. They

are not available if the loss or damage was caused by negligence.

Further, by virtue of Clause 24 the Hague Rules as enacted in the

United States Carriage of Goods by Sea Act 1936 are specifically

incorporated into the charter party. Thus to the extent that some

of the exceptions provided by Clause 16 - for example, fire -

are wider than those provided by the Hague Rules, they will be

rendered ineffective.

Baltime

Clause 13 provides (inter alia) as follows:

"The Owners   only to be responsible for delay

in delivery of the Vessel or for delay during

the currency of the charter and for loss or

damage to goods on board, if such delay or

loss has been caused by want of due diligence

on the part of the Owners or their Manager in

making the Vessel seaworthy and fitted for the

voyage or any other personal act or omission or

default of the Owners or their Manager. The

Owners   not to be responsible in any other case

nor for damage or delay whatsoever and howsoever

caused even if caused by the neglect or default

of their servants. The Owners not to be liable

for loss or damage arising or resulting from strikes,

51.

lock outs or stoppage or restraint of labour

(including the Master, Officers or Crew) whether

partial or general."

This clause gives considerably wider protection to a ship owner
than any we have seen so far. In particular, "due diligence" is
not construed as in the Hague Rules so as to include the failures
of servants, agents and independent contractors, but is qualified
by the word "personal". In other words as long as he and his
manager have personally exercised due diligence to make the vessel
seaworthy, the ship owner can rely upon this exception. This is
the case even though the ship is in fact unseaworthy - for example,
because   one of his servants or agents has failed to exercise
due diligence. Thus in Westfal-Larsen v Colonial Sugar Refining Co
[1960] 2 Lloyds 206, the vessel was unseaworthy, by reason of
having taken on board contaminated fuel oil. There was evidence
that it was the chief engineer's responsibility to examine fuel
oil before taking delivery, but there was no evidence of any
personal want of due diligence on the part of the ship owner.
Accordingly, it was held that the charterers were bound to contribute to the general average expenditure made necessary by the
chief engineer's negligence.

However, the burden is upon the ship owner to show
how the loss or damage complained of arose and that it was not
caused by want of due diligence on his part. Thus if he cannot
give an explanation of how he came to lose or damage the goods
which is consistent with there being no fault on his part, he
will be unable to rely upon the exception.

Turning to voyage charter parties, it is much more likely that the goods being shipped are those of the charterer. Again, one must look at the terms of the particular charter party to see what defences are available. However, many voyage charter parties incorporate some or all of the Hague Rules. To give you just a few examples:

(i) The Soviet Wood Charter Party 1961 and the Baltic Wood Charter Party 1964 both set out verbatim the provisions of Article IV Rules 1 and 2.

(ii) The General Ore Charter Party 1962 incorporates Article IV by reference.

(iii) The Australian Grain Charter Party 1956 incorporates Articles III (except Rule 8), IV, VIII and IX by reference.

(iv) The Grainvoy Charter Party 1966 and the Polish "Nuvoy" both incorporate Articles III and IV by reference.

However, there are two commonly used forms of voyage charter party which do not, in their standard form at least, incorporate the Hague Rules or any part of them, namely the Gencon and the Centrocon Charter Parties.

Clause 2 of the Gencon Charter Party provides:

"Owners are to be responsible for loss of or damage to the goods or for delay in delivery of the goods only in case the loss, damage or delay has been caused by the improper or negligent stowage of the goods (unless stowage performed

53.

by shippers/charterers or their stevadors or
servants) or by personal want of due diligence on
the part of the Owners or their Manager to make the
vessel in all respects seaworthy and to secure that
she is properly manned, equipped and supplied or
by the personal act or default of the Owners or
their Manager.

And the Owners are responsible for no loss or damage
or delay arising from any other cause whatsoever,
even from the neglect or default of the Captain or
Crew or some other person employed by the Owners on
board or ashore for whose acts they would, but for
this clause, be responsible, or from unseaworthiness
of the vessel on loading or commencement of the
voyage or at any time whatsoever. Damage caused by
contact with or leakage, smell or evaporation from
other goods or by the inflammable or explosive
nature or insufficient package of other goods not
to be considered as caused by improper or negligent
stowage, even if in fact so caused."

This is a very broad exceptions clause and is in many respects
similar to Clause 13 of the Baltime form. As with the Baltime
clause, the emphasis is upon <u>personal</u> want of due diligence and
again the burden of proving that the loss or damage was not caused
by want of due diligence on his part will be upon the ship owner.
In addition to Clause 2, the Gencon Charter Party contains
comprehensive strike and war clauses.

On the other hand, Clause 29 of the Centrocon Charter.
Party provides:

"The Steamer shall not be liable for loss or
damage occasioned by the Act of God, by Quaratine
Restrictions, by Perils of Sea, or other Waters,
by Fire from any cause or wheresoever occurring,
by Barratry of the Master or Crew, by Enemies,
Pirates or Thieves, or by Arrest or Restraint of
Princes, Rulers or People, by Riots, Strikes or
Stoppages of Labour, by explosion, bursting of
Boilers, Breakages of Shafts or any Latent Defects
in Hull, Machinery, or Appurtenances, by Collision,
Stranding or other Accidents arising in the
Navigation of the Steamer, even when occasioned by
the Negligence, Default or Error of judgment of the
Pilot Master Mariners or other servants or the
ship owners or persons for whom they may be
responsible (not resulting, however, in any case
from want of due diligence by the Owners of the
Steamer, or by the Ship's Husband or Manager). But
nothing herein contained shall exempt the Ship
Owners from liability for damage or loss to cargo
occasioned by bad stowage, by improper or insufficient
Dunnage, by absence of efficient ventilation, or
by improper opening of Valves, Sluices or Ports.
The Owner shall not be liable for any delay in the
commencement or prosecution of the Voyage due to a
General Strike or Lock out of Seamen or other persons

necessary for the movement or navigation of the Vessel".

As you can see, the approach adopted is very different - rather than adopting a broad blanket exemption as in the Gencon form, the Centrocon exclusion clause particularises the defences upon which the ship owner may rely. Thus it will be for the ship owner to establish, if he wishes to escape liability, that the loss or damage was caused by one or more of the excepted perils. The defences particularised are largely the same or very similar to those we have already considered.

That, ladies and gentlemen, concludes what I have to say to you today. Not surprisingly, I have not had the time to consider all of the defences which may be available, but I hope that I have illustrated some of the more important points to keep in mind should that unfortunate day come when you are faced with a claim for loss of or damage to cargo.

GENERAL AVERAGE & SALVAGE AND THE EFFECT OF FRAUD

Speaker: Douglas A Cole
Resident Partner
Richards Hogg
International Average
Adjusters Singapore
Singapore

GENERAL AVERAGE AND SALVAGE AND THE EFFECT OF FRAUD
===

The subjects of General Average and Salvage do not, I feel have
great relevance when dealing with the question of fraud. Certainly it is not common practice for anybody to try and fraudulently create a general average situation, for the returns would
be, to say the least, minimal and before any money could change
hands, the watchdogs of everybody's interests, namely the general
average surveyor and the general average adjuster would have to
be satisfied that all was above board and correct. To expand on
this a little further, it may be beneficial to briefly look at
the origins of both general average and the current day average
adjuster.

General average as a basic concept was around thousands of years
ago at the time when the phoenicians were great traders throughout the Mediterranean. In those days of sail, it was not unusual
to find that the master of the vessel was also the owner and
further that the owners of the cargo on board such vessel would
actually travel with their merchandise. Let us picture therefore
a sailing vessel travelling across the Mediterranean with all the
relevant parties to the adventure being on board and a storm breaks
and the vessel springs a leak. The master conducts an examination
of the vessel and concludes that the only way the position can be
saved is by jettisoning some of the cargo. He therefore calls
the merchants together and advises them of his appraisal of the
situation. At this stage, it is doubtful whether he would ask

for someone to volunteer for the jettisoning of their particular cargo for undoubtedly nobody would step forward. However, if the merchants knew that it did not matter whose cargo was jettisoned, as that person's losses would be made good at the end of the voyage, then of course no arguments would arise as to whose cargo should be jettisoned. Accordingly, the merchants would indeed be content for the master to make the decision as to which cargo should be jettisoned based on his seafaring judgement.

Let us assume that in our particular case, the jettisoning was sufficient to save the ship and the remaining cargo and she arrives safely at her destination. The people involved in this particular maritime adventure being commercially minded would realise that by sacrificing one set of cargo their own cargo and the ship had been saved and therefore the merchant who has suffered the loss should receive contribution from themselves towards such loss for indeed in another voyage, the roles might well be reversed. To assess the amount that each of the interests should pay, the merchants and the master might well have agreed to call on an independent trader who had previous experience in this sort of matter to come along and attend at the quayside and make his assessment. This particular gentleman could be said to be the forerunner of today's general average adjuster. This particular gentleman would examine the facts, satisfy himself as to the value of the cargo jettisoned together with the values of the property saved and make his pronouncement

as to the amounts that everybody should pay with respect to cargo lost, as well as his own fees. The various merchants and the master would then settle their respective contributions and go on their independent ways.

This very simple example contains the basic ingredients of general average and can be equated with many general average situations of today excepting of course that merchants no longer travel on board the ships. It is very unlikely that fraud could have reared its ugly head in that particular situation seeing that all the parties to the adventure were actually on board the vessel at the time of the occurrence. It is perhaps also worth mentioning at this point that we are talking about a point in time when insurance was not in being and this illustrates that general average is quite independent of insurance. The parties in the above example were merely looking at settlements between themselves and were not involved in claiming on the insurance policy. Nowadays it so happens that most insurance policies do cover general average contributions but it is important to realise that liability to contribute to general average or for that matter salvage, has no direct connection and is not dependent upon whether an interest is insured.

As trading expanded, the practice of merchants travelling with their goods gradually stopped and it also became increasingly rare for a master to be the owner of the vessel. Accordingly therefore, it became increasingly difficult to settle a general average on the quayside. There were still learned gentlemen in

various ports who could be called upon to issue statements but
the practice would obviously have developed to deal with these
matters more by way of correspondence. It also follows that
different practices would have grown up in various ports and
countries and hence merchants and shipowners would be faced
with a multitude of different laws and practices applying to
identical situations. Hence throughout the years there became
an increasing desire to standardize the adjustment of general
average but this did not really get off the ground until the
middle of the 19th century and the first set of York-Antwerp
rules were published in 1877. These have gradually been
revised with new sets of rules being issued in 1890, 1924,
1950 and the last set in 1974 and it is these latter rules
that govern the vast majority of all general average situations
that arise today by virtue of their incorporation into most
bills of ladings and/or charter parties.

The basic principles that govern general average are fairly
straightforward and can be very easily summarised as follows :-

1) The sacrifice or expenditure must be extraordinary
    in nature. This precludes ordinary voyage expenditure
    incurred merely to fulfill a contract of affreightment
    and hence shipowners cannot recover their ordinary
    expenditure under general average. This is perhaps the
    one area where the shipowner might fraudulently try and
    gain out of general average.

2) The act must be intentional and voluntary and not be
    inevitable.

3) There must be a peril and it must be real and substantial.

4) The action must be for the common safety and not just
    for the benefit of one interest. A clear example of this
    could be on a reefer ship when the refrigerating machinery
    breaks down. In an endeavour to save cargo the vessel
    puts into a port to repair the refrigerating machinery.
    Clearly the vessel herself is not in peril and the action
    can only be considered for the benefit of the cargo
    interest and hence the expenditure will not fall to be
    general average.

With the above requisites in mind, I will look at two simple
examples to illustrate the basic principles :-

1) STRANDING
    A vessel strands let us say, as a result of navigational
    error and is holed in her bottom and stuckfast on rocks.
    In these circumstances there would clearly be a peril
    insofar as the vessel is in danger of sustaining further
    damage with consequent loss and/or damage to her cargo
    and hence any action taken to save the vessel and cargo
    will be for the common safety. The costs of tugs engaged
    to assist in the efforts to refloat together with the
    expenses of lightening cargo are all extraordinary costs

and they would be voluntarily incurred. Hence all the requirements of general average are satisfied. If cargo was damaged during the lightening operations or jettisoned to assist in refloating then such losses would similarly be allowable in general average. The same would apply to any damage sustained to the vessel during efforts to refloat.

2) FIRE

A fire occurs in the cargo hold and the vessel puts into a port of refuge to enable the fire to be extinguished. Again, the necessary elements can clearly be seen to exist for obviously with a serious fire there is a peril to the property and the efforts to extinguish would be for the common safety and the expenditure incurred in entering the port of refuge and engaging the services of fire fighters are both voluntarily incurred and extraordinary in nature. Damage sustained to any of the property as a result of the extinguishing operations would also be made good in general average, but not fire damage itself.

These simple guidelines can be applied to numerous other instances of casualties occurring at sea such as collisions where serious damage is sustained, mechanical failures which either partially or totally immobilizes the vessel hence leaving her at the mercy of the elements.

Having considered the basic concepts of general average, the
question should now be asked as to whether fraud could creep
into any of these situations. Perhaps the most important
point which goes right against the basic theory of fraud is
that expenditure has actually got to be incurred and settled
prior to any recovery being made and the general average
adjuster will require to sight all the accounts and evidence
for payment and further many of these will also have to be
placed before the general average surveyor.

In view of this it is extremely unlikely that a shipowner
would gain something for nothing. I also have serious doubts
as to whether a shipowner would have sufficient knowledge
of the intricacies of general average to be able to create a
false general average situation and falsify the expenditure
in order to effect a profit. I am sure there must be easier
ways.

A general average could arise as a result of an attempted fraud
by a shipowner where for example a scuttling might be bungled
and instead of the vessel sinking she may drift ashore. All the
required elements of general average might then arise as
mentioned in the examples. If, in an attempt to cover the
attempted scuttling, the shipowner was then to refloat the vessel,
would he be able to recover in general average the ensuing expenditure and what would be the position of the innocent cargo

interests who may suffer losses as a result of such refloating operations?

Rule 'D' of the York-Antwerp rules 1974 states that the rights to contribution in general average shall not be effected, although the event that gave rise to the sacrifice of the adventure may have been due to the fault of one of the parties to the adventure, but this shall not prejudice any remedies or defences which may be opened against or to that party in respect of such fraud.

Looking at the first part of this rule, it would seem that the shipowner could recover contributions from the concerned in cargo. However, upon making such payments the concerned in cargo would then have a right of action against the shipowner which would obviously succeed. Therefore to avoid the circuity of action, the cargo interest would refuse to make the initial settlement with the shipowner. The innocent cargo who have suffered a loss as a result of the refloating operations will however be protected for he will still be entitled to receive from the other cargo interests and the shipowner, contributions towards the loss. The cargo interests who make such contributions would then bring an action against the shipowner for the recovery of such contributions. I should perhaps here also mention that the shipowner would not be able to recover this proportion of the general average expenditure from his hull and

machinery underwriters for section 66 of the marine insurance
Act 1906 states that in the absence of expressed stipulation,
the insurer is not liable for any general average loss or
contribution where the loss was not incurred for the purpose of
avoiding or in connection with the avoidance of a peril insured
against.

Cases do arise where a shipowner requests an average adjuster
to prepare a general average statement in respect of expenses
incurred at a port where the adjuster does not consider they
fall to be general average. These situtations usually arise
due to a misunderstanding of what constitutes general average
and could not be considered as an attempt at fraud. Very
occasionally however, there are blatant attempts by the shipowner to disguise the facts behind the vessel putting into a
port or the detention thereat in an attempt to obtain recovery
of his expenditure in general average. This is not a common
occurrence and any reputable adjuster and certainly any adjuster
who is a member of the Association of Average Adjusters, would
have no hesitation in refusing to proceed with the adjustment
and at the same time would notify the cargo interests of
their withdrawal from the case.

If there is very little gain involved in a shipowner fraudulently
attempting to create a general average situation there can be even
less to gain from a shipowner's involvement in salvage situations
and indeed salvors are often the people who foil attempts at

scuttling vessels and presentation of fraudulent claims.

Virtually everybody has a basic understanding of the word
salvage but as is the case in many aspects of maritime affairs,
there are finer legal definitions to specific words and this
is true of salvage. Salvage charges are defined by Section 65,
Sub-Section 2 of the Marine Insurance Act and they are the
charges recoverable under Maritime Law independently of contract.
It is clear therefore that in legal terms, to be considered as
salvage charges a payment must be made independent of any
contract and the amount must be awarded by the appropriate
court. This type of salvage is sometimes referred to as common law
salvage and nowadays is not encountered too often as the majority
of salvage work is undertaken under terms of Lloyd's open form
or other contracts such as daily rates or lumpsum price. Much
has been written as to whether salvage under Lloyd's open form
is indeed salvage under contract but nowadays the point in only
of academic interest for under the York-Antwerp Rules 1974,
Rule 6 salvage, whether under contract or not, is to be included
in general average.

For any shipowners and/or insurers who are present, I would
just digress slightly and point out that problems can arise
on claims on hull and machinery policies due to the fine legal
definitions of salvage charges due to the fact that some
policies with limited conditions do include the wording to cover
salvage charges and as mentioned, this would only therefore

include salvage not under contract.

Strictly speaking, salvage under contract would either fall
to be general average or sue and labour charges, depending
on the circumstances. I have come across many instances
where clearly the intention was to cover the shipowner for
expenditure incurred in the nature of salvage without limiting
it to those charges strictly in accordance with the fine legal
definition but due to a misunderstanding of the exact terminology,
the required cover has not been given.

To return to the main subject of salvage and fraud it sometimes
happens that a well meaning salvor puts in a timely appearance
just when a vessel is being scuttled, which can lead to an
interesting exchange of rapid messages between the respective
masters. Let us take an example where the sea cocks have been
opened and the crew have abandoned ship and the salvage tug
then arrives on the scene and is successful in salving the
vessel. The salvor would have a maritime lien on the salved
property and would exercise that lien until such time as satis
factory security is provided. It is important to note that if
cargo was on board the vessel they would have to provide security
to the salvor even though they were a completely innocent party.
It follows of course that the concerned in cargo would be liable
to the salvor for their proportion of the salvage award and will
then have to bring an action against the shipowner for the recovery of the amount that they pay. The same position applies

where a salvage takes place under the terms of a Lloyd's open form for when a master signs such a form he binds each interest separately to pay for their respective proportions of the award and consequently the cargo interest would have to settle with the salvor and then seek to recover his outlay from the shipowner. Salvage under Lloyd's open form is on the basis of 'No Cure No Pay' and obviously this basis applies to common law salvage, and therefore no payments are due unless the property is saved and further before a shipowner could recover the salvage charges from his insurers he would have to settle such and hence there could not possibly be any element of profit in it for the shipowner. Obviously of course if the necessity for salvage charges arose as a result of the wrongful action of the assured no claim would arise on the insurance policy.

It will be seen therefore that salvage, if anything, helps to prevent losses by fraud and in no way assists in the presentation of fraudulent claims.

I hope what I have said throws a little light on general average and salvage and shows that they are not two subjects that you really need to concern yourselves with when looking at the question of Maritime Fraud.